# Contents

## Dear Traveler

I am a traveler first and a writer second. I put together these guides because I have found the information so useful in my own travel. My focus is providing the information that curious traveler's might find useful on road trips, particularly that which isn't often available in other guide books. I love the off the beaten path places, the unique, the less trodden, the roads that often go where most people don't go, and I love to know more about history, culture, background, geology, geography, what have you. But in my many travels down these roads I have often been frustrated by a lack of gathered information about how to get there, the quality of the road itself, where a nearby grocery, laundromat, park or bathroom might be found, and just general practical traveler information. So, I've tried to provide an (almost) comprehensive look at these places for other travelers like myself.

But there is a caveat I want to share with readers who might be more familiar with commercial guide books. I don't have an editor. I travel, research, write and publish these on my own. And, it shows. While I attempt to be scrupulous about the accuracy of the information I provide, I'm not so good at the editing and formatting part. And, ultimately, I've decided not to worry too much about it. When I'm looking for the address of a restaurant I don't really care if it comes before or after the phone number in one listing and is reversed in another. I don't care if the entry is bold or italicized or in 14 or 16 font. And, I'm making the assumption that you, dear reader, will also overlook these and other formatting mistakes. These guides are incredibly time consuming to create, and I'd rather spend the time doing the travel, research, and writing and share that information than spend the time editing. So, for those of you who are sticklers for spelling or formatting, I apologize in advance. You are going to find mistakes in your reading. My hope is that the mistakes don't ever get in the way of getting to where you want to go.

And, some mistakes are actually not my fault. Places move, addresses get misprinted on flyers or menus, places close, etc. Please feel free to email me if you have any information that will help improve the accuracy of the entries in the book (mvasudeva03@yahoo.com). I know I would appreciate it and I imagine the reader will as well.

Happy Travels!

## Introduction to this Guide

The focus of this Road Trip Guide is an (almost) comprehensive listing of the unique, the useful, the inspiring, the intriguing, the interesting that makes this area worth visiting. It does not include chain restaurants or lodging (with a few exceptions. If a chain is the only place in the area to eat or sleep, then it's listed).

## Organization of the Guide

The guide is organized around the counties included, starting with I90 in the North of the state to the Sawtooth Recreation Area in the South (and a kind of arbitrary line from the recreation area to Oregon on the West and to Montana on the East). I've picked this central region because it's beautiful and a great destination and because it's often ignored or given very short shift in other guidebooks.

## Introduction to the Region

Central Idaho is a largely rural area abundant with National Forest lands, mountain ranges and rivers, but the small quaint towns and state and federal land that make up the area are worth visiting, with excellent outdoor recreation. Culture and history also make an appearance, with a particular emphasis on Lewis and Clark and First Americans. This guide's focus is on this less known part of Idaho, nestled between the popular Coeur d'Alene on the Washington and Idaho border and the trendy Sun Valley in the South and the populous Boise to the southwest. There are no cities included, with Coeur D'Alene and Moscow on the West side the biggest towns you'll encounter. As you traverse the central area, you'll understand why. This is mountainous terrain with few flat spots and often few paved roads. Don't worry though, you can still get around with a bit of planning and without too much trouble, and you will be rewarded by spectacular, almost untouched wilderness.

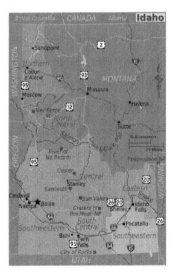 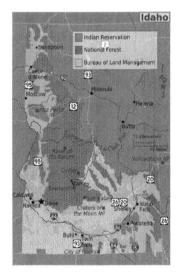

## Idaho Maps

(Creative Commons license from Wikitravel, {{Imagecredit|credit=Peter Fitzgerald,wmc:User:25or6to4|captureDate=9 June 2009|location=Idaho|source=Image:Idaho regions map.svg|caption=Idaho regions map|description=English version}}{{Map|Idaho}}

*Practicalities*

- Visitor Information

  Road Conditions, 511.idaho.gov

  Ski Conditions,
  http://www.skiidaho.us/conditions?gclid=COSq_saz6LwCFYeEfgod5V4AeQ

  General Travel Info: www.visitidaho.org

  www.visitnorthcentralidaho.org

  visitnorthidaho.com

  Idaho Centennial Trail  Trail travels 900 miles through Idaho. For detailed
  information, check out the Idaho parks and rec brochure
  http://parksandrecreation.idaho.gov/sites/default/files/uploads/documents/centen
  nialtrail/Centennial%20guide%20pdf.pdf

    Another trail guide is available at
    http://idahoptv.org/outdoors/shows/centennialtrail/maps.cfm

- Audio Tours

  A variety of audio tours are offered through Tourist offices and the Forest
  Service. Stop at Idaho Department of Parks and Recreation offices and Forest
  Service Ranger Stations to ask about availability.

- Winter Activities

  Glacier Country Avalanche Center, www.glacieravalanche.org

  Flathead Avalanche Center, www.flatheadavalanche.org

- Biking

  Idaho is a biking Mecca. There are few, if any, states that have developed as
  many bike trails that interconnect literally across the state. You could ride from
  the Idaho/Canada border to the Idaho/Nevada or Utah or Wyoming or Oregon
  Border.

  *Media Connection: A map of the state ke routes is available at*
  *http://www.itd.idaho.gov/bike_ped/BikeMap2010.pdf*

- Birding

Birding is very popular throughout this part of Idaho and Idaho Fish and Game has created maps of birding trails with lists of birds to be sited at Idaho Birding Trail, http://fishandgame.idaho.gov/ifwis/ibt/default.aspx

*Media Connection: The Idaho Birding Trail Guidebook is available as a hard copy for $5 from any Idaho Dept of Fish and game office*

- Fishing

A valid fishing license is required for all types of fishing for those over 14. Visitors can get license and tag information online and purchase a license online at http://fishandgame.idaho.gov/public/licenses/?getPage=68

Get additional fishing information from the following sources:

> Idaho fishing, see this website http://fishandgame.idaho.gov/public/fish/
> Fishing on the Flathead Indian Reservation, 406-675-2700,
> cskt.org/trlfwrc.htm
> If you are fishing on Indian Reservation waters, a separate license is
> required

*Kids Alert*

*Check out the website, www.visitidaho.org/children-in-nature/, if you are bringing kids with you to Idaho.*

## Getting Oriented

- The area included in this guide starts with Kootenai county just N of I90 down to just N of Boise, Ketchum and Sun Valley. The area includes almost all of the Bitterroot Wilderness that is in Idaho.

- Flying: Those hoping to fly to the area can fly into Spokane, Washington or to Boise, Idaho Falls or Hailey Idaho.

- Amtrak (800-USA-RAIL) runs through the northern section of the area with stunning views.

# Kootenai County

## Practicalities

- Visitor Information

www.kcgov.us

- Boat Launch Pass, planning on launching a boat? Get your pass online at http://www.kcgov.us/departments/parkswaterways/launchpermit.asp

## Getting Oriented

- Kootenai County is located in the Panhandle of Idaho. The largest city in the area is Coeur D'Alene.

- I90 comes in from Washington and exits into Montana at the S edge of the county.

## Spirit Lake GPS: 47.58N, 116.51W ; Elevation: 2569ft

## Getting Oriented

- The railroad used to bring passengers to Spirit Lake around 1910. The lake was not just a vacation destination but also used to float logs to the local mill. In 1930, a forest fire was almost the end of the town, and it descended into a long, slow decline. Today Spirit Lake has a mix of closed and open store fronts in its small downtown.

- W of Hwy. 95 at the intersection of Hwy. 54 and 41, Spirit Lake sits on the North side of the lake in the Northwest corner of the county near the Washington border. Maine St allows access to the lake.

## Practicalities

- Visitor Information

  www.spiritlakechamber.com

- Grocery

  Miller's Harvest Foods, 31964 N 5th Ave, 208-623-4751, harvestfoodsnw.com, full service grocery with deli, bakery and wine shop

- Library

  Spirit Lake Library, 32575 N 5th Ave, 208-623-5353

## Shopping

- Spirit Lake Books and Coffee, 31911 N 5th Ave, 208-623-6409, www.spiritlakebooks.com, 9am-6pm, closed Sun, coffee, books, sandwiches

## Activities

- Spirit Lake City Park, , Maine to Spirit Lake Rd, boat launch, public beach

- Spirit Lake, from Hwy 41, take Resort Rd to Silver Beach

  The 12 miles of shoreline makes Spirit Lake a popular vacation spot. Public Access to the lake at Bronze Bay (10892 W Carroll Rd), Main St Launch,

## Dining

- Annie's Country Kitchen, 32471 N 5th St, 208-623-2206, 6am-2pm

  Homemade traditional meals like pancakes, burgers, corned beef hash,

- Fourth and Main Pizza, 6185 W Maine St, 208-623-6246, 4thandmainpizza.com, facebook page updated regularly, 11am to close, closed Sun.

  Family owned pizza and gelato, salads, soup and sandwiches where all food is made on-site.

- La Sierra, 6249 W Maine St, 208-623-2532

  Mexican food

- The Parkside, 6249 W Maine St, 208-623-2799, www.theparksidesl.com, wine and beer, under $10

  Diners step back in history when they enter the Parkside with black and white photos of local lumber and logging history lining the walls. A big screen tv, a baby grand and occasional live music liven up the casual, recently renovated space. Very small menu of sandwiches.

- Spirit Lake Books and Coffee, 31911 N 5th Ave, 208-623-6409, www.spiritlakebooks.com, 9am-6pm, closed Sun, coffee, books, sandwiches

  Bagels, sandwiches, pastries and cookies in a book lined room.

- White Horse Saloon, Grill & Hotel, 6248 W Maine St, 208-623-2353, 10:30-9pm, opens at 8am on Sat and Sun, under $15, indoor and outdoor dining

  Full American menu with pasta, burgers, salads and sandwiches in the 1907 saloon.

## Camping

- Sedlmayers Resort, 6843 Spirit Lake Rd, 208-623-6863, www.sedlmayers.com, RV sites, lakehouse for rent, picnic tables, boat launch, fishing, hiking

## Lodging

- Silver Beach Resort, 9724 W Spirit Lake Rd, 208-623-4842, www.silver-beach-resort.com, cabin rentals, boating, fishing, hiking, swimming, $55-115, bedding is not provided

  Water front cabins are rustic, historic with simple decor, wood walls and rag rugs on the floor. Wood burning stoves provide heat.

- White Horse Saloon, Grill & Hotel, 6248 W Maine St, 208-623-2353, 8 rooms, $40-60

## Rathdrum GPS: 47.48N, 116.53W ; Elevation: 2211 ft

*Getting Oriented*

- Rathdrum  feels like a suburb of Coeur d'Alene with the towns running together at Rathdrum's S side.

- West of Hwy. 95 at the intersection of Hwy. 53 and 41 and just NW of Coeur d'Alene. Rathdrum Peak is visible to the Northwest of the town. Twin Lakes is to the North on Hwy 41.

*Practicalities*

- Visitor Information

  Rathdrum Area Chamber of Commerce, 8184 W Main St, 208-687-2866, rathdrumchamberofcommerce.com

- Grocery

  Stein's IGA, 16102 Hwy. 41, 208-687-1341

  Super 1 Foods, 15837 Westwood St, 208-687-4480, super1foods.net

- Restrooms

  Rathdrum Library, 16320 Hwy. 41, 208-687-1029

*Parks*

- John Brown Playfield, 15574 N Washington, playground

- Majestic Park, 5750 W Majestic Ave, 208-687-2399, water park play area

- Rathdrum City Parks, 15456 N Latah St, playground, picnic tables

- Rathdrum Skate Park, 7851 Main St, sun up to sun down

- Roth Park, 14475 N. Roth Court off Hwy. 41, picnic area

- Stub Myers Park, 8320 W 4th St, walking path, playground, picnic tables

- Thayer Park, 6896 Winchester, off Pine, playground

*Activities*

- Old Kootenai Museum, 802 2nd At, www.rathdrumhistory.com

Set in the original jail from 1890, the museum has been restored to serve as a museum and archive focused on North Idaho's past.

*Coffee*

- Java Junction, 15618 Hwy. 41, 208-687-9032

- Jitterz, 14480 N Hwy. 41, 208-687-3847, gone?

- Laughing Latte, 14480 Hwy. 41, 208-687-3847

*Dining*

- Burger Heaven, 13735 Hwy. 53, 208-687-2211

  Pizza and burgers

- The Country Nook, 13668 Hwy. 53, 208-687-8480

- Granny's Pantry, 14683 Hwy. 53, 208-687-0881, 7am-8pm, seasonal opening

  Large red booths and comfortable decor serving comfort food

- Joey T's Taste of Chicago, 16102 Hwy. 41, 208-687-5639, 10-7pm

  Hot dogs, Gyros and Italian Sausage

- Kelsey's, 13785 W Hwy. 53, 208-687-3748, www.kelseys.ca, chain

- O'Malley's Sports Pub & Grill, 762 W Hwy. 53, 208-687-5996

  Fish and chips, burgers and other pub favorites

- San Francisco Sourdough, 15963 N Hwy. 41, 208-687-2207, www.sfsourdougheatery.com, deli chain

- Toro Viejo Restaurant, 15837 N. Westwood Dr, 208-867-3723, www.toroviejo.com

  Local Mexican chain

- Wah Hing Restaurant, 15512 Hwy. 41, 208-687-1688

  Chinese American food

- Zip's Drive In, 14480 Hwy. 41, 208-687-9144, zipsdrivein.com

  Burgers, fish and chicken served with crinkle cut fries

*Lodging*

- Twin Echo Resort, 24045 N Lakeview Blvd, 208-687-1045, winechoshores.com,

  Rustic lakeside cabins

- Cedar Springs Bed and Breakfast, 6734 W Sturgeon Rd, 208-687-9333, www.cedarsprings-bb.com, cabins, 5 rooms, hot tub, $65-150

  Large deck and living room can be used by guests. Floral spreads and neutral furnishings.

## Hauser  GPS: 47.46N, 117.1W ; Elevation: 2215 ft

*Getting Oriented*

- Access Hauser from Hwy. 53 on N Hauser Lake Rd. Hauser is a few miles S of Hauser Lake and near the Idaho/Washington border.

*Practicalities*

- Grocery

  Hauser Market and Smoke Shop, 26913 W Hwy. 53, 208-773-5571, mobil.com

*Activities*

- Hauser Lake park and launch, 10702 N Faye Pl, Hwy. 53 to N. Hauser Lake Rd to N. Fay Rd, Rt, playground, swimming beach, restrooms

*Dining*

- Curley's Hauser Junction, 26433 W Hwy. 53, 208-773-5816, curleys.biz, 10am-2am, indoor and outdoor dining, live events, pool tables, several dining areas

  This is quite a spread serving a menu of almost all fried foods with a few salads and pizza. Decor is old West style.

- Dinki Di's Hauser Lake Resort, 18226 W Main St, 208-773-3987

- Kirk's Espresso, 26837 W Hwy. 53, 208-777-1289, drive through

## Coeur D'Alene  GPS: 47.41N, 116.46 W ;  Elevation: 2152 feet

*Learn More About it: Coeur D'Alene means Heart of Awl in Iroquois, and it is believed that this name comes from David Thompson, a Northwest Fur trader in the 1800's. Thompson hired some Iroquois as guides and scouts and they described the First People's in this area as having very sharp trading practices, like the heart of an awl. The local first people's used the name "Schee-Chu-Umsh" to name themselves.*

*Getting Oriented*

- Coeur d'Alene is 40 miles directly East of Spokane on I90. Hwy. 95 runs north/south through Coeur d'Alene. The City sits on the north side of Lake Coeur d'Alene with I 90 running across the north side, turning south at the east edge of the city. Hwy. 95 comes in from the west side, crosses the inlet and then turns into Lincoln Way

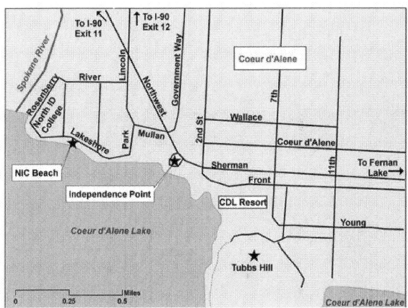

## Map of Coeur d'Alene

fishandgame.idaho.gov

*Practicalities*

- Visitor Information:

Gateway Northwest Visitor Center, 105 N First St, 877-782-9232, 9am-5pm, restrooms, picnic area, information center about Coeur d'Alene and all of Northwest Idaho and Northeast Montana. Access to Centennial trail.

Coeur d'Alene Field Office, 3815 Schreiber Way, 208-769-5000, 7:45-4:30 M-F

Fernan Ranger Station, 2502 E Sherman Ave, 208-664-2318

facebook.com/cdacvb, updated regularly

coeurdalene.org

- Restrooms

  Boardwalk Marina, 115 S 2nd St

  Coeur d'Alene City Park, west of downtown on the waterfront

- Grocery

  Pilgrim's Market, 1316 N. 4th St, 208-676-9730, www.pilgrimsmarket.com, 9am-9pm, natural and organic products, deli

  Albertsons, 220 W Ironwood Dr, 208-664-9101

  Costco Coeur d'Alene, 355 E Neider Ave, 208-676-7360

  Safeway, 1001 N 4th St, 208-664-6019, 101 W Neider Ave, 208-765-4311

- Laundry

  Laundry & Cleaning Village, 1136 N 4th St, 208-765-8900

  Cleando Laundry Center, 179 W Haycraft Ave, 208-664-0804

Lake Coeur D'Alene

## Parks

- Bluegrass Park, 6071 N Courcelles Pkwy, northwest side of the city, picnic areas, playground, water area, bike trails, disc golf, restrooms

- Coeur D'Alene City Park and Beach, Access on Northwest Blvd and Mullan Rd, west of downtown on the waterfront, 16 acres of picnic areas, playground and access to Centennial Trail, skate park, BMX track, Restrooms.

- Fernan Open Space Park, 2751 E Potlatch Hill Rd, 54 acre open space park with one mile of shoreline. Park is currently undeveloped

- Higgens Point Park and Cocoeur d'alene Lake Coeur d'Alene Lake Dr, off Coeur d'Alene Lake Dr just W of I90, accessible from Coeur d'Alene Lake Dr and Centennial dr, requiring a 5min walk, restrooms, picnic area, boat launch

  Park and then walk up hill to the top of the point where there is a shaded picnic area and great views. From Higgins to Coeur d'Alene is a long park that is mainly a bike/walking trail (part of the North Idaho Centennial Trail). Runs along the lake. Higgins point park has boat launch facilities.

- McEuen Park, 420 E Front St, currently closed for construction

- Mica Bay, boat access campground, Putnam Rd to Tall Pines Rd, 7m south of Coeur d'Alene, restrooms, hiking trails, picnic area, camping, no running water

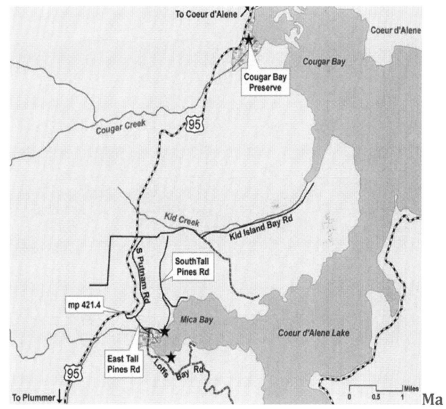

**p of Mica Bay and Lake Coeur d'Alene**

(courtesy of fishandgame.idaho.gov)

- Riverstone Park, 1805 Tilford Lane, picnic area, bike and walking paths, playground, restrooms, access to the Prairie Trail, a spur of the North Idaho Centennial Trail

*Guides and Tours*
- Wine Tours, Beverly's 7th Floor of Coeur d'Alene Resort, 208-765-4000, daily at 4:30

- Crystal Gold Mine, 51931 Silver Valley Rd Exit 54 I90, Historic Kellogg, 208-783-GOLD, www.goldmine-idaho.com, 9-6 summer, 10-4 winter, $12-45

- Coeur d'Alene Audubon, www.cdaaudubon.org, facebook page

  Regular events and talks are offered and listed on the website or on the facebook page

- Sierra Silver Mine, 420 5th St, 208-752-515, silverminetour.org, 10-4pm summer, 10-2 winter, $14-45

*Biking*
> *Media Connection, map of bike trails, (not very good)*
>
> *http://www.cdaid.org/files/Parks/Trails/Trails%20Main/All%20Trails%20an d%20Bikeways%202011.pdf*
>
> *Bike Brochure,*
> *http://www.cdaid.org/files/Parks/Trails/Trails%20Main/brochure.pdf*

- Terra Sports, 510 Sherman, 208-765-5446, www.terrasportsinc.com, bike rentals starting at $35 for half day

- Vertical Earth, 2175 N Main St, 208-667-5503, www.verticalearth.com, rental bikes starting at $15, also rents bike carriers

*Hiking*
> *Media Connection, map of trails*
>
> *http://www.cdaid.org/files/Parks/Trails/Trails%20Main/All%20Trails%20an d%20Bikeways%202011.pdf*

- Coeur d'Alene Parkway, 5.7m paved parkway (part of the Centennial Trail) that runs along the lake in Coeur d'Alene accessible on E Coeur d'Alene Lake Dr.

- Tubbs Hill, 210 South 3rd St, several miles of hiking trails, restrooms. Mudgy Moose Trail is in Tubbs Hill (mudgyandmillie.com).

  > *Media Connection: The city of Coeur d'Alene has a variety of brochures and maps for Tubbs Hill*
  >
  > *Map of Tubbs Hill:*
  > *http://www.cdaid.org/files/Parks/parks/Tubbs%20Hill/Tubbs%20Hill%20Ma pbook%20Overview%20flat.pdf*

*Historical and Nature Brochure:*
*http://www.cdaid.org/files/Parks/parks/Tubbs%20Hill/TubbsBrochuresmalle*
*r.pdf*

- Mineral Ridge National Recreation Trail, 3.3m, 11m East of Coeur d'Alene, take I90 east for eight miles to Wolf Lodge Bay exit and then south on Hwy. 97 for 3m, picnic area, pit toilets.

  *Media Connection. Trail guide with map and detailed information is accessible at*
  *http://www.blm.gov/id/st/en/visit_and_play/places_to_see/coeur_d__alene_fie*
  *ld/Minaeral_Ridge_National_Recreation_Trail.html*

- North Idaho Centennial Trail, 24m mostly paved trail for bikes and walks, travels from Higgins Point 6m E of Coeur d'Alene to the Idaho/Washington border, www.northidahocentennialtrail.org

  *Media Connection: for map,*
  *http://www.northidahocentennialtrail.org/files/4313/3519/8026/nictf-*
  *membership_application-online.pdf*

- Prairie Trail, 1810 W Tilford Lane, Riverstone Park, 4m spur for the North Idaho Centennial Trail

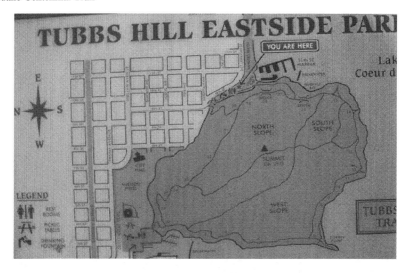

# Map of Tubbs Hill

*Boating and Rafting*

- Downtown Waterfront, downtown you can find seaplane rides, parasail rides, jet skis, kayaks, paddleboats and canoes for rent.

- Coeur d'Alene Paddleboard Company, 512 Sherman Ave, 208-292-4156, cdapaddleboard.com, facebook page updated regularly, rentals and lessons, paddleboard yoga

- Blackwell Island Recreation Site, S on Hwy. 97 across the Spokane River and then right, 5am-11pm (gated), seasonal, boat launch, fee, picnic sites, flush toilets, potable water, pets on leash, 1/4m trail

- Boardwalk Marina, 115 S 2nd St, 208-415-5600, www.hagadonemarine.com/marinas/rental-boats, small motor boats, pontoon boats, wakeboard school

- Fresh Water Fun, 10201 W Rockford Bay Rd, 15 minutes south of Coeur d'Alene, 509-688-3934, www.freshwaterfun.com, pontoon boat rentals.

- Lake Coeur d'Alene Cruises, 115 S 2nd St at the Coeur d'Alene Resort, 208-765-4000, www.cdaresort.com, daily cruises including family themed options

- Harrison Pontoons and Rentals, 629 E Harlow Point Rd, 208-696-1770, harrisonpontoons.com, 8:30-7pm, boat rentals and vacation rentals

- Kayak Coeur d'Alene, 307 E Locust Ave, 208-676-1533, www.kayakcoeurdalene.com, rentals ($40-85 half to full day), and classes

- Just Add Water Sports (JAWS), 1010 E Sherman Ave, 208-765-8333, cdajaws.com, boats, jet skis and pontoon rentals.

  *Learn More About It: The Lake was created over 10,000 years ago from glacial meltwater. It covers 32 miles in length and has more than 40 bays.*

*Horseback Riding*

- Rider Ranch, 6219 S Wolf Lodge Creek Rd, 208-667-3373, www.riderranch.com, hour ride starts at $45, evening dinner ride starts at $60

  Working ranch with trail rides and hayrides.

- Coeur d'Alene Adventures, 208-918-2082, cdaadventures.com, $40 for 90min

*Fishing*

- Row Adventures, 202 E Sherman Ave, 208-770-2517, www.rowadventures.com, fly fishing

- Fins and Feathers Tackle Shop and Guide Service, 1816 Sherman Ave, 208-667-9304, www.fins1.com, guide service and bait and tackle shop.

*Skiing*

- Silver Mountain Resort, 610 Bunker Ave, Kellogg, 35 miles from Coeur d'Alene, 208-783-1111, silvermt.com, skiing, snow boarding and snow tubing in winter; golf, hiking, fishing and rafting in summer.

*Scenic Drives and Byways*

- Lake Coeur d'Alene, 35.8m one way, begins at I90 and Hwy. 97 and travels south along the shoreline of Lake Coeur d'Alene with many bird viewing areas and hiking trails

## Map of Lake Coeur d'Alene Scenic Byway

*Amusement Parks*

- Silverwood Theme Park and Boulder Beach Water Park, 27843 N hwy. 95, Athol, 208-683-3400, silverwoodthemepark.com, 11-9, theme park; 11-7 water park (seasonal), $20-40

- Raptor Reef Indoor Water Park/Triple Play Family Fun Park, 175 W Orchard Ave, Hayden Lake, 208-762-7529, www.3play.com/raptor-reef, 25,000 sq ft facility features a wave pool, children's lagoon, miniature golf, bowling, go karts and a climbing wall.

## Cultural and Historical Attractions

- Museum of North Idaho, 115 Northwest Blvd, 208-664-3448, www.museumni.org, 11-5 Tues-Sat April to Oct, $3 adults, $7 families, museum store, walking tours ($15) offered at 11am at Old Fort Sherman and at 1:30 in downtown,

  Museum focuses on the west expansion at the end of the 19th century including exhibits on steamboats, railroads, stage lines, gold mining and the Coeur d'Alene tribe.

- Coeur D'Alene Summer Theater, North Idaho College, 208-769-7780, cdasummertheatre.com

- Lake City Playhouse, 1320 E Garden Ave, 208-667-1323, lakecityplayhouse.org

- Coeur d'Alene Symphony, 1042 W Mill Ave, 208-765-3833, www.cdasymphony.org

- Devin Galleries, 507 Sherman Ave, 208-667-2898, www.devingalleries.com, a rotating selection of artwork

- The Art Spirit Gallery, 415 Sherman Ave, 208-765-6006, www.theartspiritgallery.com, fine art and fine craft by established artists

- The Coeur d'Alene Galleries, Coeur d'Alene Resort Lobby, 208-667-7732, cdagalleries.com, historical artists and contemporary art featured

## Natural Attractions

- Cougar Bay Preserve, I90 exit 12, Hwy. 95 2m, 208-267-8999, www.nature.org/ourinitiatives/regions/northamerica/unitedstates/idaho/placesweprotect/cougar-bay.xml, 1-5m hiking trail, canoeing, kayaking, bird watching

  88 acre preserve bordered by coniferous forests and including lush meadows on the edge of a mountain lake, animals and birds are drawn here.

## Shopping

- Shoo Fly Fishing Co, 1010 E Missoula Ave, www.shooflyfishingtackle.com, 406-295-8495, fishing tackle shop

- Stein's Market, 607 E Missoula Ave, 406-295-4177, www.steinsmarket.com, 6am-11pm, grocery, deli, bakery, fish and game licenses

*Activities*

- Frontier Ice Arena, 3525 W Seltice Way, 208-765-4423, www.frontiericearena.org, see online schedule, $5 public skate

*Wine, Beer and Cocktails*

- Barrel Room No. 6, Coeur d'Alene Cellars, 3890 N Schrieber Way, 208-664-2336, cdacellars.com, 12-8, closed Sun-Mon., summer concert series, check website for info.

*Coffee and Tea*

- *Java Coffeehouse and Cafe, 324 Sherman Ave, 208-667-0010, javaonsherman.com, serves Stumptown coffee

  coffee, pastries, egg and bagels and even French toast make up a large breakfast menu. Lunch includes classic sandwiches, paninis and salads. Also a nice late afternoon snack menu.

- Calypsos Coffee and Creamery, 116 E Lakeside Ave, 208-665-0591, www.calypsoscoffee.com, roasting beans onsite, wifi, art, 7am-9pm

  Comfortable coffeehouse with living room style decor. Full breakfast and lunch are served include soup and salad specials. Ice cream is available.

- Bakery by the Lake at Parkside, 601 East Front St, 208-415-0681, pmmtt.com/BBTL, 6am-5pm, see under bakery above

- McFarland Inn Afternoon Tea, 208-667-1232, www.mcfarlandinn.com/dining-teas/afternoon-teas.htm, $18 for full tea, by reservation only

*Dining*

- **For a Fun Meal**

- Rogers Burgers, 155 W Neider Ave, 1224 E Sherman Ave, 208-664-0696, rogersburgers.com, 10:30-10pm, meals under $10

  Fresh cut Idaho potatoes, ground beef, turkey and veggie burgers as well as premium ice cream for sundaes, shakes or malts.

- **Family Friendly**

  - Tomato Street, 221 W Appleway Ave, 208-667-5000, www.tomatostreet.com, 11-9pm

    Italian food in a friendly family atmosphere with a sports bar

- **For Pizza**

- Fire Artisan Pizza, 517 E Sherman Ave, 208-676-1743, fireartisanpizza.com, 11-10pm

  Rustic, casual atmosphere

- MacKenzie River Pizza Co, 405 W Canfield Ave, 208-772-5111, mackenzieriverpizza.com

  Rustic, upscale atmosphere with a large variety of choices.

- **For a Treat**

  - Roger's Ice Cream and Burgers, 1224 E Sherman Ave, 208-930-4900

    155 W Neider Ave, 1224 E Sherman Ave, 208-664-0696, rogersburgers.com, 10:30-10pm, meals under $10

  - Coeur D'Alene Chocolates, 3650 N Government Way, 208-667-0107, cdachocolates.com

  - Jamm's Frozen Yogurt, 3500 N Government Way, 208-665-0485, jammysyogurt.com, 10am-10pm

- **For Breakfast**

- Garnet Cafe, 315 E Walnut Ave, 208-667-2729,

  Classic breakfast dishes with unusual twists and some not so classic dishes like breakfast spaghetti. Omelets, corned beef hash, green eggs and ham, oatmeal and other breakfast gems are served in this tiny, off the beaten path downtown cafe. Often a wait.

- Michael D's Eatery, 203 E Coeur D'alene Lake Dr, 208-676-9049, micaelds.com, 6am-2pm

  Lots of egg dishes, pancakes, biscuits and gravy and oatmeal.

- Jimmy's Down the Street, 1613 E Sherman Ave, 208-765-3868, jimmysdownthestreet.com, 5:30-2:30

  Made from scratch home cooking with southern flavors. Big pecan sticy buns, chicken fried steak and biscuits and gravy.

- Jonesy's, 819 E Sherman Ave, 208-666-1641, jonesyscda.com, 6am-2pm

  Large helpings of freshly made breakfast goodies including pancakes, omelets, oatmeal and lunch choices like tuna melt and cheeseburgers. If you are really hungry, try the triple decker Club.

- The Breakfast Nook, 1719 N 4th St, 208-667-1699, runooked.com, 6am-2pm

    Traditional breakfast foods in a traditional diner.

- **For Baked Goods**

- Pastry and More, 411 W Haycraft Ave, 208-667-3808, www.pastryandmore.com, 7am-5:30pm, closed Mon,

    From scratch bakery with lunch sandwiches and soup as well.

- Bakery by the Lake cafe, 601 E Front Ave, 208-415-0681, pmmtt.com/BBTL, 6am-close

    Light breakfast and lunch options, bars, buns and cupcakes, and coffee.

- **For a Game**

    - Mulligan's, 506 W Appleway Ave, 208-765-3200, bwcdainn.com/mulligans/

        Comfort food in a sports bar casual atmosphere

    - Capones Sports Pub and Grill, 751 N 4th St, 208-667-4843, caponespub.com, 11am-11pm

        Beer garden and lots of tvs for sports events. Also serves a full menu including lots of craft beers.

- **Ethnic Food**

    - Santorini's Greek Cuisine, 4055 N Government Way, 208-676-0401, facebook page, 11-3 Mon-Wed, 11-8 Thu-Sat

        More upscale Greek serving a full menu of Greek meals as well as Greek beer and wine.

    - Olympia Restaurant, 301 E Lakeside Ave, 208-666-9495, facebook page updated regularly, 11-8pm, Greek

        Gyros and fries and other traditional Greek options in a small Greek themed restaurant.

    - Taco Works, 510 E Best Ave, 208-704-2091, 8am-7pm, tiny little taco truck

        Pork tacos, chicken nachos, veggie burrito at good prices.

    - Bonsai Bistro, 101 E Sherman Ave, 208-765-4321, www.bonsaibistro.com, 11-10pm

Pan Asian and Sushi.

- Mexican Food Factory, 1032 N 4th St, 208-664-0079, mexicanfoodfactory.net, facebook page, 5:30am-8:30pm, indoor and outdoor seating, drive thru

  Breakfast burritos in the morning, traditional mexican platters for lunch and dinner.

- Syringa Cafe, 1401 N 4th St, 208-664-2718, syringasushi.com, 11:30-4 Mon, 11:30-9 Tues-Fri, 4-10 Sat, closed Sun.

  Sushi and Japanese cafe

- **For Lunch**

- Cafe Carambola, 610 Hubbard St, 208-676-8784, 11-3, facebook page

  Eclectic cafe with a variety of ethnic cuisines including Mexican, Brazlian, African and Latin American.

- Best Sandwich Shack, 512 Best Ave, 208-625-0629, 11-8pm, sandwich truck

  Cheesesteak

- Meltz Extreme Grilled Cheese, 1735 W Kathleen Ave, 208-664-1717, meltzextreme.com, 11-7pm

  Grilled cheese but other options as well including a buffalo chicken sandwich, soups, and frito pie.

- Bent's Pitchamps BBQ, 510 E Best Ave, 208-215-6021, facebook page

  Pulled pork and chicken, ribs with ten sauce options, potato wedges and slaw served from a food truck.

- *Scrud's Gourmet Grub, 206 N 4th St, 208-667-6000, facebook updated regularly, 11-9pm, closed Sunday

  Burgers, fresh cut fries, chicken sandwiches, wings and some really unusual sandwiches including a gringo special with green chile, sausage and pepperjack. Also serve shakes. Check out the facebook page for the special.

- Franklin's Original Cheesesteak Hoagies, 501 N 4th St, 208-664-3998, www.franklinshoagies.com, 7am-8pm, 8am-3pm on weekends

  Breakfast include a Philly cheeseteak omelet as well as traditional favorites and for lunch Original cheesesteak and a variety of other sandwiches.

- Hudson's Hamburgers, 207 E Sherman Ave, 208-664-5444,

   Old school burger joint serving burgers and only burgers.

- Herbie's Deli, 4055 N Government Way, 208-667-8840, 10-3pm, closed Sun

   Wide variety of sandwiches in a casual deli setting. Serves turkey and avocado, turkey and cranberry, grilled wraps corned beef and other traditional sandwiches.

- **For a View**

- Dockside Restaurant, 115 S 2nd St, 208-765-4000, www.docksidecda.com

   Comfortable turquoise booths overlooking the lake. For breakfast, some really unusual options include homemade cake donuts and wild huckleberry fritters, trout with eggs and hashbrowns, and cream caramel french toast as well as usual breakfast options. Lunch features a big salad bar soup and sandwiches and traditional comfort food including mac and cheese, meat loaf and fish and chips.

- Cedars Floating Restaurant, 1 Marina Dr, 208-664-2922, www.cedarsfloatingrestaurant.com, 4pm, full bar, indoor/outdoor dining

   You'll have to walk the plank to get to the restaurant sitting in the lake. Steaks, Salmon, King crab and rack of lamb served with salad bar and bread.

- Tony's on the Lake, 6823 E Coeur d'Alene Lake Dr, 208-667-9885, tonysonthelake.com, 4pm

   Upsacle Italian restaurant with traditional Italian food including Osso Buco, Eggplant parmesan, and breaded chicken cutlet. Fettuccini alfredo and lasagna.

- **For Casual Dinner**

- Scrud's Gourmet Grub, see under lunch

- Bardenay, 1710 W Riverstone Dr, 208-765-1540, www.bardenay.com, full bar

   Idaho chain serves innovative casual food

- Fisherman's Market And Grill, 215 Kathleen Ave, 208-664-4800, fishermansmarketcda.com, 11-8pm, closed Sun.

   Emphasis is on fresh fish with a variety of fish and chips options and seasonal menu items.

- Wolf Lodge Steakhouse, 11741 E Frontage Rd, 208-664-6665, www.wolflodgerestaurants.com, 5-12pm

  Rustic decor with tall wood booths in a stone and wood tack room style restaurant. Steak and fish heavy menu. Dishes are served with salad, potato, beans and bread.

- Tito's Italian Grill and Wine Shop, 210 Sherman Ave, 208-667-2782, titomacaroni.com, lunch, dinner and togo, children's menu, full bar

  Soup, pasta and pizza with some Italian apps (many of them fried), and for dinner full entrees. Large wine selection.

- The Beachouse, 4316 Coeur d'Alene Lake Dr, 208-664-6464, www.beachousecda.com, indoor and outdoor, full bar

  Casual, water's edge restaurant heavy on fish and meat served with rolls and potato.

- Mulligan's, 506 W Appleway Ave, 208-765-3200, bwcdainn.com/mulligans/

  Comfort food in a sports bar casual atmosphere

- **For Upscale Dinner**

- Angelo's Ristorante Italiano, 846 N 4th St, 208-765-2850, angelosristorante.net, 5-10pm

  Traditional Italian menu

- Bistro on Spruce, 1710 N 4th St, 208-664-1774, www.bistroonspruce.com, 9am-9pm, Sunday until 3pm, wine and beer

  Cozy atmosphere with stone fireplace and an unusual menu for this area. Expect upscale preparations of traditional food including a Guinness Onion soup, a smoked salmon flatbread or Sushi grade tuna. Tapas is also available.

- Beverly's Restaurant, 115 S 2nd St,, 208-765-4000, beverlyscda.com,

  Upscale dining room overlooks the lake through floor to ceiling windows, granite floors and copper ceilings. Seafood bar, a variety of game options, and house cured charcuterie in addition to a few traditional options. Organic and sustainable products used when possible.

- The Cellar, 313 Sherman Ave, 208-664-9463, thecellarcda.com, 11:30-

Brick walls, a full bar and upscale ambience make for a fine dining experience. start with a plate of olives, bread and crostini or crab croquettes followed by soup or salad and a small selection of entrees, pizza and pasta.

- Greenbriar Inn, 315 E Wallace Ave, 208-667-9660, greenbriarcatering.com/, 3pm, closed Sun-Mon, full bar

Full dinner and tapas menu in dining room with fireplace, deck and patio seating.

- Scratch Restaurant, 501 E Sherman Ave, 208-930-4762, scratchspokane.com, 11-10pm, closed Sun.

    Pretty eclectic menu, probably one of the more unusual in town. Here you'll find a variety of ethnic favorites including hot pot, buffalo burger, flat iron steak and grilled tenderloins. Some vegan and vegetarian options.

- 315 Martinis and Tapas Dinner, 315 E Wallace Ave, 208-667-9660, www.315martinisandtapas.com, 9am-11pm, indoor and outdoor eating, full

    1908 Inn houses this lovely restaurant. Tapas style menu with a variety of small plates, mostly under $10 including brushcetta, Ahi, lettuce wraps and edamame. Some larger entrees are also available.

- Seasons of Coeur d'Alene, 209 Lakeside Ave, 208-664-8008, seasonsofcda.com, full bar

    Bright lights and neon decorate the contemporary dining room with a full bar and a smaller, quiet lounge. Pub like food including a burger, chicken club and polenta tart.

- Bonsai Bistro, 115 S Second St, 208-765-4321, see under ethnic restaurants

## Camping

- Lake Coeur d'Alene Camping Resort, 10588 E Wolf Lodge Bay Rd, 208-664-4471, www.campcda.com, fishing, boating, hiking, boating and swimming, seasonal

    Full hook up RV sites, tent sites and cozy cabin rentals

- Wolf Lodge Campground, 12329 E Frontage Rd, 208-664-2812, www.wolflodgecampground.com, I90, exit 22, seasonal, wifi, laundry, canoe rental

    RV sites, campgrounds, cabins in shaded spots with a grassy playground. Nightly campfire

*Bed and Breakfast*

- Abbotswood House, 3620 N Honeysuckle Dr, 208-667-5608, www.abbotswoodhousebandb.com, indoor pool, outdoor hot tub, $125, air con

  Authentic English bed and breakfast with full gourmet breakfast, a game room, some rooms with fireplaces. Only two rooms are booked at any one time. Rooms range from simple twin beds to larger suite like rooms with sitting areas. Decks and patios open the house to the outdoors.

- American Country Bed and Breakfast, 705 S Zircon Ln, 208-651-2191, americancountrybedandbreakfast.com, wifi, $145-215

  Adult only lodging with country decor on a 5 acre property with a large shared deck and a 24/7 snack area. Rooms feature lush furnishings and antiques. A separate "treehouse" outside offers unique lodging (but the bathroom is a lighted walk outside to the main house).

- Blackwell House Boutique Hotel, 820 Sherman Ave, 208-765-7799, www.blackwellboutiquehotel.com, hot tub, $160-225

  Contemporary decor, hard wood floors and billiards table and media room give this bed and breakfast a clubby atmosphere. The rooms are set in a craftsman home with modern decor. There is nothing frilly about this lodging that emphasizes blacks, whites and grays.

- Ida Home Bed and Breakfast, 16310 W Riverview Dr, 208-773-6169, www.ideahomebnb.com, four rooms, wifi, hot tub, fire pit, shared and private bath, $148

  Large open great room for guests to share on a 5-acre park like setting. Rooms are luxuriously decorated with

- McFarland Inn, 601 E Foster Ave, 208-667-1232, www.mcfarlandinn.com, wifi, bicycles, 5 rooms, $155-165

  Elegant bed and breakfast set in a large Craftsman home in the Garden District. Rooms feature floral spreads, light colors and lots of light. Gourmet breakfasts are served in the sunroom.

*Casual Lodging*

- Lots of chains in Coeur d'Alene with a few specialty options

- The Coeur d'Alene Resort, 115 S 2nd St, 208-765-4000, www.cdaresort.com

  Views of the lake in some units. Several restaurants on site and many activities.

*Upscale Lodging*
- Greenbriar Inn, 315 E Wallace Ave, 208-667-9660, greenbriarcatering.com/lodging/, $85-150

  Suites and rooms with a common area for visitor use. Rooms feature wrought iron beds and upscale furnishings. The house itself is a large restored historic home with a wrap around deck, sunrooms, garden and a gazebo.

- Roosevelt Inn, Spa and Event Center, 105 E Wallace Ave, 208-765-5200, $149-359

  Once a school house, this upscale inn emphasizes historic elegance and luxurious rooms and suites. Large wood headboards, brocade bedding and attention to detail in all the rooms.

## Post Falls GPS: 47.71N, 116.94W ; Elevation: 2182 feet

*Getting Oriented*
- I90 runs through Post Falls. The Spokane River runs to the S of the Interstate, just past downtown. The Washington/Idaho border is at the West side of town.

*Practicalities*
- Visitor Information

  www.visitpostfalls.org

  www.postfallsidaho.org

- Restrooms

  Post Falls Library, 821 N Spokane St, 208-773-1506

  Most public parks (see below)

- Laundry

  Laundromat, 702 N Spokane St, 208-773-9282

  Seltice Laundry & Dry Cleaning, 2450 E Seltice Way, 208-773-1115

- Grocery

  Super 1 Foods, 805 E Polston Ave, 208-777-0607, super1foods.net

  Rosa's Italian Market & Deli, 120 E 4th Ave, 208-777-7400, rosasmarket.com

*Parks*

- Beck Park, 2610 N Howell Rd, playground, restrooms, 2 loops paved walking paths make up about one mile

  9 acre park

- Black Bay Park, 1299 E 3rd Ave, S end of N Bay St, fishing, hiking, restrooms

  Paved trails connect to the Centennial Trail

- Chase Sports Field Complex, 410 W 21st Ave, playground, half mile path

- Corbin Park, 896 S Corbin Rd, picnic areas, river access for fishing and rafting, restrooms, disc golf

- Falls Park, 305 W 4th St, off W. 4th Ave on the N side of the river, picnic shelters, restrooms, interpretive signs, playground

  22 acre park with the Spokane Valley Irrigation Canal. Park is set along the dam

- Kiwanis Park, 4176 E Weatherby Ave, picnic areas, restrooms, playground, swimming beach, trails

  40 acre park with several loop trails ranging from half to full mile, making for a total of 2.5m

- Millennium Skate Park, 300 N Greensferry Rd,

- Post Falls Arboretum, off 5th between Spokane and Idaho St.

  50 species of trees with interpretive signs

- Q'emiln Riverside Park and Trails, 12201 W Parkway Dr, off S Spokane St on the S side of the river, swimming beach, boat launch, picnic areas, restrooms

  4 miles of hiking trails along the Spokane River gorge. Small trails can be combined or done separately leading to a variety of historic sites and homesteads. Rock climbing also on site.

## Map of Q'emiln Park Trail System

- Singing Hills Park, 1015 Teton Ave, playground, paved trail, no dogs

- Syringa Park, 2975 N Bunchgrass Dr, playground, picnic, restrooms, walking paths

- Treaty Rock Park, 705 N Compton St,

  Large flat, granite outcropping with pictographs that might be the signing of a treaty. Some people believe that the rock was the site of the treaty signing between Chief Seltice and Fredrick Post, the town founder. A trail loops through the park.

- Woodbridge Park, 705 N Silkwood Dr., playground, restroom, .5m walking path

*Activities*

- Buck Knives Tour, 660 South Lochsa St, 800-326-2825 for reservation, tours are free and offered Mon-Thurs at 10, 12 and 2pm

- River Queen Cruises, 414 E 1st Ave, 208-777-1414, www.templinsmarina.com/river_queen.asp, cruises are offered in the season at various times. See website for offerings, $49 for an adult.

- Frontier Ice Arena, 3525 W Seltice Way, 208-765-4423, www.frontiericeareena.org

- Jacklin Center of Arts and Culture, 405 N Williams St, 208-773-4389, www.thejacklincenter.org,

  Music, theater and a variety of classes are offered.

- Post Falls History Walk, www.postfallshistorywalk.webs.com

List of historic sites and description

- Spokane River Centennial Trail, 37m  North Idaho Centennial Trail of which ten miles run through Post Falls

  The trail runs between Post Falls Idaho and Nine Mile Falls Washington. The trail is fully paved.

- Post Falls Historical Society, 101 E 4th Ave, 208-262-9642, fee, historic artifacts

## Coffee and Tea

- Coffee Cottage, 1115 N Spokane St, 208-773-8059, facebook updated regularly, wifi, 5:30-7pm, indoor and outdoor seating

- Doma Coffee Roasting, 6240 E Seltice Way, 208-667-1267, domacoffeee.com, 7:30-4pm,

- Java the Hut, 501 E Seltice Way, 208-773-8369, 5am-6pm, drive through

- Kokopelli, 3915 E Poleline Ave, 208-773-0641, facebook page updated regularly, 5:30-5pm includes some breakfast items like yogurt, bagels

- Leopard Lattes, 220 N Spokane St, 208-773-8141, facebook page updated regularly, drive through

- Mugsy's espresso, 1604 E Seltice Way, 208-773-3723, 5am-6pm

- Thomas Hammer Coffee Roasters, 3904 E Mullan Ave, 208-457-9531, www.hammercoffee.com, espresso bar

- Post Falls Coffee Co and Bakery, 801 W Seltice Way, 208-660-1179, pfcoffee.com, wifi, drive up and sit in

  Coffee drinks and pastries in a casual, comfortable setting suitable for hanging out

## Beer, Wine and Cocktails

- Bi Plane Brewing Company, 4082 E Primrose Ln, 208-683-0369, biplane brewing.com, 11-8pm, closed Mon. May not be open anymore

- Enoteca Fine Wine and Beer, 112 E Seltice Way, 208-457-9885, www.corkjoy.com, 11am-late, Sun 12-5, wine and beer tasting and retail

- Selkirk Abbey Brewing, 6180 E Seltice Way, 208-292-4901, www.selkirkabbey.com, 3pm-7pm, 1-8pm on Fri and Sat, closed Sun

Belgium themed brewery

- Stateline Plaza, 7200 W Seltice Way, 208-777-7778, convenient mart and restaurant

Wine tasting, draft beers, Sunday ticket

*Bakery*
- Sweetwater Bakery, 119 E 3rd Ave, 509-326-0806, www.sweetwaterbakery.com

Everything is made from scratch from pastries and cookies to bagels

*Dining*
- Big Bear Deli, 700 E 8th Ave, 208-457-8465

Cold cut sandwiches and salads

- Cabin Restaurant, 4041 W Riverbend Ave, 208-773-3086

Fish and chips, chowder in a homey atmosphere

- Capone's Pub and Grill, 315 S Ross Point Rd, 208-457-8020, caponespub.com, 11am-11pm

Pizza, sandwiches, soup and salad

- Famous Willies Barbecue, 107 E 7th Ave, 208-773-0000, facebook page updated regularly, 11am-8pm

- Fleur de Sel, 4365 Inverness Dr, 208-777-7600, fleur-de-sel.weebly.com, 5pm to close, closed Sun-Mon, under $25, indoor and outdoor dining

Upscale, attractive restaurant with white table cloths and artfully designed food. One of the nicest restaurants in town.

- Fu-ki Japanese Steakhouse and Sushi, 1500 E Seltice Way, 208-457-7077, www.fukisteakhouse.com, 11:30-3, 5-9:30, all day on weekends, most dishes under $25

Steakhouse and Sushi bar with freshly prepared food. Chef prepares the sushi in front of guests.

- GW Hunters Steakhouse, 615 N Spokane St, 208-777-9388, gwhunters.com, 6am-9pm

- La Cabana Mexican Restaurant, 604 E Seltice Way, 208-773-4325

- La Cocina, 780 N Cecil Rd, 208-777-1280, 11:30-8

  Authentic Mexican food in large servings

- Mallards Restaurant, 414 E 1st Ave, 208-773-1611, www.redlion.com, 6:30am-9pm

  At the Red Lion Hotel and with river views. Serves American classics.

- Nates New York Pizza, 920 N Hwy. 41, 208-773-6697, natesnewyorkpizza.com, website didn't work, facebook page updated regularly, 11-8pm, under $25

  Pizza by the slice, whole pizzas, sandwiches and salads.

- Old European, 1710 E Schneidmiller Ave, 208-777-2017, www.oldeuropean-restaurant.com, 7am-2pm, under $10

  Carefully prepared European style dishes. Big servings of home cooked fare like Dutch babies and crepes, Turkey sandwiches, biscuits and gravy and cinnamon rolls, or for lunch dishes like Hungarian Goulash.

- Oval Office Bistro and Martini Bar, 620 N Spokane St, 208-777-2102, whitehousegrill.com, facebook page, 11am-11pm, under $25

  Fish, lamb, burgers in an attractive contemporary setting. Some unusual flavors compliment the fresh food.

- Rancho Viejo, 2525 E Seltice Way, 208-773-6600, www.rancho-viejo.net, 11am-10pm

  Brightly colored and decorated space with familiar Mexican favorites

- Ricardo's Baja Tacos, 504 E Seltice Way, 208-620-0132, www.ricardosbajatacos.com, 7am-7:30pm, under $10

  Small restaurant serving tacos and burritos made fresh

- Sahara Pizza, 801 W Seltice Way, 208-773-7733, saharapizza.com, 11am-10pm, delivery

  Chain pizza

- Templin's Marina Bar and Grill, 414 E 1st Ave, 208-777-1414, templins.redlion.com, 11-8, in summer

  Hamburgers, fish and chips, hard ice cream, salads right on the river

- Toro Viejo, 3960 W 5th Ave, 208-667-7876, www.toroviejo.com

  Small, local chain of Mexican food

- Tree of Life, 565 North Vest, 208-773-2865, facebook page updated regularly, 10-5pm, closed Sat., under $10

  Relaxing, family oriented dining and bakery. Sandwiches and Salads with a Jewish emphasis including Reubens with the corned beef made onsite. Soups are made daily.

- White House Grill, 712 N Spokane St, 208-777-9672, whitehousegrill.com, 11am-10pm, under $20

  Mediterranean food with a big garlic emphasis like potatoes smothered in garlic, roasted garlic served with walnuts and cheese, salads, gyros and beef.

- Zips Drive In, 3927 W Riverbend Ave, 208-457-8444, www.zipsdrivein.com

  Small chain serving burgers, fries and chicken

*Lodging*
- Chains in town include Red Lion, Comfort Inn, Sleep Inn

- Ida Home Bed and Breakfast, 16374 W Riverview Dr, 208-773-6169, idahomebnb.com, 4 rooms, shared and private bath, wifi, hot tub, fire pit, full breakfast, $128-250

  Large great room and deck for guest use. Rooms are large and spacious, decorated with sturdy, dark antiques and luxurious bedding

- River Cove Bed and Breakfast, 212 S Parkwood Pl, 208-773-1014, www.therivercove.com, wifi, hot tub, full breakfast, 1 and 2 bedroom suites, rooms, $129

  Suites with fireplaces and waterfront views are decorated in pastel colors. A yacht is also available for the night. Large living room and deck for guest use. Grounds connect to the centennial trail.

- Riverbend Inn, 4100 W Riverbend Ave, 208-773-3583, riverbend-inn.com

  Standard motel

- SilverStone Inn and Suites Post Falls, 3647 W 5th Ave, 2088-829-3124, chain

## Hayden GPS: 47.45N, 116.47 W ; Elevation: 2287 feet

*Getting Oriented*

- Downtown has a nice old-time feel with locally owned shops

- N of I90 on Hwy. 95, just W of Lake Hayden.

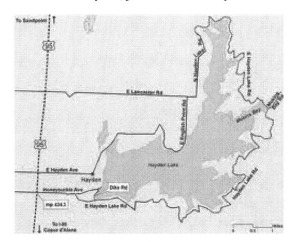

## Map of Hayden Lake
(courtesy of fishandgame.idaho.gov)

*Practicalities*

- Visitor Information

    Web: haydenchamber.org

- Grocery

    The Flour Mill Natural Foods, 88 W Commerce Ave, 208-772-2911, facebook page, 9am-5pm,

    Super 1 Foods, 240 W Hayden Ave, 208-772-5722

    Walmart, 550 W Honeysuckle Ave, 208-209-4044

- Laundromat

    Cleanco Laundry & Dry Cleaning, 200 W Hayden Ave, 208-772-0310

- Library

Hayden Lake Library, 8385 N Government Way, 208-772-5612, 10am-8pm

*Parks*
- Croffoot Park, 1347 W Lancaster Rd, Lancaster and Ramsey Rd

  25 acre park mostly game fields

- Finucane park, 550 E Prairie, Prairie Ave and Fourth St, playground, restrooms

  10 acre park

- Hayden City Park, 8930 N Government Way, playground

- Honeysuckle park, Honeysuckle Ave, swimming beach with lifeguard, boat launch, picnic areas, restrooms, fishing dock

*Activities*
- Triple Play Family Fun Park, 175 W Orchard Ave, 208-762-7529, www.3play.com, family fun and water park

  Bowling, climbing wall, arcade, bumper boats, laser tag and miniature golf in addition to an indoor water park featuring a wave pool and children's lagoon.

- Hayden Lake, access from the S on E Hayden Lake Rd and from the N on Lakeview Dr

  40 miles of shoreline and 4000 acres in size nestled beneath timbered mountains make this a beautiful setting for outdoor recreation, and the lake's popularity should come as no surprise.

*Fishing*
- Hayden Lake Marina, 3830 E Hayden Lake, 208-762-0181, haydenlakemarina.com, gas, convenient store

  Boat rentals

*Dining*
- Blue Plate Cafe, 10015 N Government Way, 208-772-8399, facebook page, 6am-1:30pm, under $10

  Simple, greasy spoon fare for breakfast and lunch that is often crowded

- The Boathouse Restaurant, 3799 E Hayden Lake Rd, 208-772-5057, boathousehayden.com, 11am-10pm, indoor and outdoor dining, most dishes under $20

Views over the marina in a comfortable, wood furniture and rustic decor. Menu emphasizes fish but also includes ribs, steak and chicken.

- Capone's, 9520 N Government Way, 208-762-5999, caponespub.com

- Carusos, 113 W Prairie Shopping Center, 208-762-4676, 7am-8pm, chain deli

- The Donut House, 8761 N. Government Way, 208-635-5288, facebook page updated regularly, open 24 hours

- Envision Cafe, 9225 N Government Way, 208-762-8488, facebook page, 7am-8pm

  Comfortable setting for coffees and cookies

- Grandma Zulus, 11050 N Government Way, 208-762-1201, 7am-2, facebook page updated regularly

  Big, Grandma like breakfasts including grits, ham and eggs and biscuits and gravy

- Noodle Express, 301 W Prairie Ave, 208-762-8488

- Owl Cafe, 9178 N. Government Way, 208-772-4912

  Breakfast all day, chicken fried steak, burgers and other comfort food. Try the stuffed hashbrowns for breakfast.

- Pita Pit, 271 W Prairie Ave, 208-772-7600

- Porch Public House, 1658 E Miles Ave, 208-772-7711, wedonthaveon.com/the-porch/, full bar, 11am, under $20

  Full menu of sandwiches, soup, salads and entrees prepared from scratch in a casual pub like atmosphere

- Qudoba Mexican Grill, 245 West Prairie Shopping Center, 208-762-9377

- Razzle's Bar and Grill, 10325 N Government Way, 208-635-5874, website doesn't work, 11am-12pm

  Burgers, Karaoke, darts and pool

- Temptations Cupcakes, 105 W Prairie Shopping Center, 208-762-5700, temptationsitsallgood.com

  Cupcakes made on site and take away to bake scones.

- Toro Viejo, 9075 N. Government Way, 208-772-0291, toroviejo.com, Mexican chain

- Wild Cat Pizza, 85 W Prairie Ave, 208-762-WILD, wildcatpizzakellogg.com, 11-9, until 11pm on Fri/Sat., delivery, under $20

*Camping*
- Alpine Country Store & RV Park, N 175 6 8 Hwy. 95, 208-772-4305, www.nirvpark.com, 25 sites, complete hookups, water, restrooms, showers, picnic area, laundry

- Mokins Bay Campground, Lancaster Rd 5m to Hayden Lake then 11 miles around the lake to the bay, 15 sites, fee, hookup, dumping, water well, pit toilets, boat launch,

- Sportsman's Park, 15649 N. Sportsman Park Rd, Lancaster Rd to the East Park Rd, boat launch, boat ramp, pit toilet, picnic tables

*Lodging*
- Chains in town include Holiday Inn

- Clark House, 5250 E Hayden Lake Rd, 208-772-3470, clarkhouse.com, 8 rooms with private baths, $225-249,  wifi

  Very elegant inn once the home of F. Lewis Clark sits on 10 acres of spacious lawns overlooking the lake. Rooms are spacious and have period decor.

- Hayden's Inn, 9986 N Government Way, 208-772-4414, www.haydensinn.com

  Typical motel

# Athol GPS: 47.56N, 116.42W ; Elevation: 2392 feet

*Getting Oriented*
- West of Hwy. 95.

*Practicalities*
- Library

  Athol Public Library, 30399 N. 3rd St, 208-683-2979

- Grocery

  Little Town Market, 6101 Hwy. 54, 208-683-7065, littletownmarket.com, 7am-9pm

*Activities*
- Hoodoo Valley, Hwy. 95N 4m to Granite Lake Rd left 1 mile and turn left on Kelso Lake Rd, birding area

- Silverwood Theme Park & Boulder Beach Water Park, 27843 N Hwy, 95, 208-583-3400, www.silverwoodthemepark.com

  Largest amusement park in the NW. Large variety of rides and attractions including four roller coasters and a water park.

*Dining*
- Country Boy Cafe, 6160 Hwy. 54, 208-683-2363, facebook page, 8am-9pm

  Small town diner serving traditional comfort food specialties like Chicken Fried Steak.

- Saddle Up Steakhouse, 5751 E Hwy. 54, 208-683-0516, facebook page, 3pm-9pm, closed Sun and Mon

  Steak, baked potatoes and salads

- White Pine Country Cafe, 30625 N Hwy. 95, 208-683-4408

  Burgers, sandwiches

- Espresso Yourself, 29629 N Hwy. 95 at Vera Ave, drive through

  desserts

*Lodging*
- Cedar Mountain Farm Bed & Breakfast, 25249 N Hatch Rd, 208-683-0572, cedarmountainfarm.com, 4 units, wifi, breakfast, laundry, $125-165

  Hand crafted log cabins in a farm setting. Hiking trails. Rooms are simple and comfortable.

- Log Spirit bed and breakfast, 31328 N Tiara Ln, 208-683-4722, www.logspirit.com, $140-200

  Great room and large patio for guest use. Rooms are simple with lodge pole pine decor and attractive prints. Decor is limited. Some rooms with hot tub.

**Bayview** GPS: 47.58N, 116.33 W ; Elevation: 2069 Ft

*Getting Oriented*

- From Hwy. 95, Bayview is E on Hwy. 54 on the SW side of Lake Pend Oreille

*Practicalities*

- Grocery

  McDonald's Hudson Bay Resort, 17813 E Hudson Bay Rd, 208-683-2211, 6am-6pm, small selection of groceries, sundries

  Bayview Mercantile, 34135 W Main Ave, 208-683-2216

- Visitor Information

  www.bayviewidaho.org

*Activities*

- Farragut State Park, 13550 E Hwy. 54, 208-683-2425, museum, beach, trail system

  40 miles of trails including the hike up Bernard Peak. Museum at the Brig has a collection of memorabilia from the Farragut Naval Training station

- McDonald Hudson Bay Resort, 17813 E Hudson Bay Rd, 208-683-2211, www.madcondladsresort.com, 6am-6pm, boat rentals,

- Scenic Bay Marina and JD's Resort, 17173 E Pier Rd, 208-683-2243, www.bayviewmarinas.com

*Dining*

- Bay Cafe, 34171 N. Marietta Rd, 208-683-2424

  Broasted chicken and fries with homemade coleslaw as well as a selection of sandwiches, burgers and pizza.

- Captain's Wheel Resort, 16908 E Pier Rd, 208-683-6504, facebook page, 11am-2am, under $20

  Burgers, fish and chips and lots of great fried stuff.

- Ralph's Coffee House, 16716 Almas Ct, 208-683-2218, ralphscoffeehouse.com website didn't work), wifi

*Camping*

- Farragut State Park, 13550 E Hwy. 54, 208-683-2425, 61 sites, 10 camping cabins, flush toilets, showers, dumping, boat launch, beach, trail system for biking and hiking

- Lakeland RV Park, 20139 Perimeter Rd, 208-683-4108, 33 sites, hook ups, drinking water, showers, pull thru sites, fishing

*Lodging*

- Scenic Bay Marina and JD's Resort, 17173 E Pier Rd, 208-683-2243, www.bayviewmarinas.com, motel rooms, camping, RV, boat launch, wifi

  Simple motel rooms

- Lighthaus bed and breakfast, 16798 E Cape Horn Rd, 208-683-0737, www.lighthausbb.com, wifi, hot tub,

  Rooms are simple with light wood furnishing and white linens

- McDonald Hudson Bay Resort, 17813 E Hudson Bay Rd, 208-683-2211, www.madcondladsresort.com, 6am-6pm, wifi, cabin rentals, boat ramp, air con, convenient store on site

  Cabins, with 1, 2 or 3 bedrooms, are set on the lake with small patios on the lake. Kitchens in all units.

- Dromore Manor Bed and Breakfast, 17216 E Cape Horn Rd, 208-683-9311, www.dromoremanor.com, $150-190

  Frilly, floral decor with antiques fits the Victorian home with a large front porch.

## Conkling Park GPS:47.24N, 116.45W ; Elevation: 2208 ft

*Getting Oriented*

- Conkling Park is on the West side of Chatcolet Lake. Conkling Rd exit off Hwy. 95.

*Activities*

- Conkling Resort and Marina, 20 W Jerry Lane, 208-686-1151, www.conklingmarina.net, RV sites, tents, cottage, restaurant, boat launch, kayak rentals, swimming, fishing, video arcade, convenient store

*Dining*

- The Steamboat Grill, 20 W Jerry Lane, 208-686-1151, www.conklingmarina.net, at the Conkling Resort and Marina, under $15

  Menu includes steak, shrimp, chicken, burgers and salads.

*Lodging*

- Conkling Resort and Marina, 20 W Jerry Lane, 208-686-1151, www.conklingmarina.net, RV sites, tents, cottage, restaurant, boat launch, kayak rentals, swimming, fishing, video arcade, convenient store

## Rockford Bay GPS: 47.30N, 116.52W ; Elevation: 2192 ft

*Getting Oriented*

- West side of Lake Coeur d'Alene on W Rockford Bay Rd

*Practicalities*

- Grocery

  Black Rock Marina, 10201 W Rockford Bay Rd, 208-664-6931, marinaatblackrock.com, boat rental, boat launch, general store

- Restrooms

  Black Rock Marina, 10201 W Rockford Bay Rd, 208-664-6931, marinaatblackrock.com, boat rental, boat launch, general store

*Activities*

- Black Rock Marina, 10201 W Rockford Bay Rd, 208-664-6931, marinaatblackrock.com, boat rental, boat launch, general store

*Dining*

- Shooter's Bar & Grill, at Black Rock Marina, 10201 W Rockford Bay Rd, 208-667-6106, marainattheblackrock.com, indoor and outdoor dining with a deck overlooking the bay

  Hand tossed pizza, salad, burgers, steak, ice cream

## Setters nothing here

## Worley GPS: 47.23 N, 116.55 W ; Elevation: 2661 ft

*Getting Oriented*

- Hwy. 95 runs through Worley, to the W of Lake Coeur D'Alene

*Practicalities*

- Corner Market, 9714 W F St, 208-686-8032

*Parks*

- Worley City Park, between 2nd and 3rd and G St

*Activities*
- H2H Bison Ranch, 30585 S Ditimore Rd, 208-775-6102, www.h2hbisonranch.com, buy bison meat, take a tour, RV spaces

  Contact the ranch for tour options

*Dining*
- High Mountain Buffet, in the casino, 7am-9:30

- Sweetgrass Cafe, in Casino, 11-8:30, opens at 8am on weekends

  Comfort food

- Chinook Steak Pasta and Spirits, in the Casino, 4-8:30, closed Mon-Tues

  Handmade pasta and pizza in a casual, comfortable setting

*Camping*
- H2H Bison Ranch, 30585 S Ditimore Rd, 208-775-6102, www.h2hbisonranch.com, RV spaces with water, sewer and hook up

- Worley City Park, between 2nd and 3rd and G St, 25 sites, electric, pets allowed

*Lodging*
- Sun Meadow Resort, 30400 S Sunray Trail, 208-686-8686, www.sunmeadow.org, nudist resort for families, cabins, camping

- Coeur D'Alene Casino Resort Hotel, 37914 South Nukwalqw, www.cdcasion.com

  Gets a lot of bus tours from Canada

## Mica Bay GPS: 47.35N, 116.51W; Elevation: 2539 ft

*Getting Oriented*
- Mica Bay is just S of Coeur d'Alene off Hwy. 95 to W Kidd Island Rd E to S Tall Pines Rd, on Lake Coeur d'Alene

*Activities*
- Mica Bay Boater Park, accessible only by boat 7m S of Coeur d'Alene, developed campground with drinking water, picnic area, vault toilet

- Mica Bay Boat Launch, 8340 S Tall Pines Rd, boat dock, vault toilet

## Harrison GPS: 47.26N, 116.46W ; Elevation: 2205 ft

*Getting Oriented*

- East side of the lake where it intersects Coeur d'Alene River, off Hwy. 97

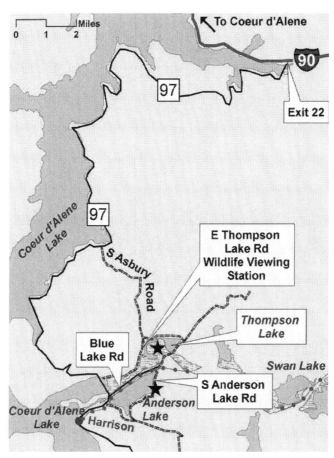

## Map of Harrison
(Courtesy of fishandgame.idaho.gov)

*Practicalities*

- Visitor Information

  www.harrisonidaho.org

- Grocery

  Hutton's General Store, 17497 Hwy. 97, 208-676-1215

  Pizza, ice cream

Harrison Trading Co, 101 S Coeur d'Alene, 208-689-3211, 8am-7pm, grocery, liquor, deli, donuts

- Restrooms

Harrison Library, 111 S Coeur D'Alene, 208-689-3976

Carlin Bay Boat Launch, 33911 S Hwy. 97, restrooms

*Events*
- Concert series, summer, sponsored by the Harrison Chamber of Commerce

*Parks*
- Harrison City Park, 200 Lake Ave, 208-689-3212, playground, picnic area

*Boating*
- Harrison is a boating Mecca with several public boat launch sites and docks. For dock reservations contact Kootenai County parks and waterways starting Jan 1st, docks fill up quickly http://www.kcgov.us/departments/parkswaterways/reservations/reservationspermit1.asp

- Carlin Bay Boat Launch, 33911 S Hwy. 97, restrooms

- Gateway Restaurant & Marina, 250 W Harrison St, 208-689-3902, www.harrisondocks.com, 11-8pm April-Sept., boat slip rentals, gas station

- Harlow Point Boat Launch, 1400 E Harlow Point Rd

- Harrison Pontoons and Rentals, 208-696-1770, www.harrisonpontoons.com, fishing boats and kayaks for rental

- Harrison Boat Launch, currently closed for construction

- Harrison Idaho Water Adventures, 250 W Harrison St, 208-582-0177 harrisonboatrentals.com, ski boat, pontoon, wave runner, paddle board, kayak, canoe rentals. Kayak tours, $65 half day.

- Hi Water Adventures, 208-582-0177, www.harrisonboatrentals.com, powerboat, jet ski, paddleboard, kayak rentals

*Activities*
- Crane Historical Society, 201 S Coeur d'Alene Ave, cranehistoricalsociety.org, noon-4pm seasonal, free

Artifacts and memorabilia on early settlers

*Media Connection: If history interests you, "The Road Less Traveled Through the Coeur d'Alenes" is a great historical introduction and driving tour through Benewah, Kootenai and Shoshone Counties, by Dorothy Dahlgren and Simone Kincaid, 2007*

- Lou's Sightseeing Cruises and Marine Services, 208-818-2254, www.captain-lou.com, bicycle shuttle services, lake cruises

  Will shuttle bikes by auto or by boat

- Pedal Pushers, 101 N Coeur d'Alene Ave, 208-689-3436, www.bikenorthidaho.com, wifi

  Bike rentals and repair

- Thompson Lake Wildlife Refuge, Blue Lake Rd, 208-769-1414

  Both Thompson and nearby Anderson lake are part of the WMA. large flocks of waterfowl migrate through this area. Thompson Lake has the largest population of nesting osprey in the western states. Drive the seven mile loop road

- *Trail of the Coeur d'Alene's, 72m paved trail that runs from Mullan to Plummer. In Harrison, the trail runs right along the lake. It's a 7m ride/walk south to historic Heyburn State Park, across the causeway and another 10 m to Plummer. This is one of the nicest, most attractive legs of the ride.

*Beer, Wine, Cocktails*
- Sheppard Fruit Wines, 102 N Coeur d'Alene Ave, 208-689-9463, www.sheppardfruitwines.com, seasonal 12-5

  Wines are made from regional fruit sources including blackberries and elderberries but they tend not to be sweet with a more balanced, dry flavor.

*Dining*
- Carlin Bay Resort, 33911 S Hwy. 97, 208-689-3295, seasonal,

  Burgers, pub food

- The Creamery, 206 S Coeur d'Alene Ave, 208-689-9241, facebook page, seasonal, hard ice cream

- Gateway Restaurant & Marina, 250 W Harrison St, 208-689-3902, www.harrisondocks.com, 11-8pm April-Sept.

  Homemade soup, pasta

- Gig's Landing, 204 S Coeur d'Alene Ave, 208-689-9400, may be gone

- Harrison Trading Company, 101 S Coeur d'Alene Ave, 208-689-3211, deli

- The Pack Rat, 130 E Frederick Ave, 208-689-3183, www.thepackrat.net, coffee and hot beverages

- Pedal Pushers, 101 N Coeur d'Alene Ave, 208-689-3436, www.bikenorthidaho.com, 8am-5pm, coffee and snacks

- The Tin Cup, 200 S Coeur d'Alene Ave, 208-689-3088, to go

  Coffee, Quiche, soup, fruit and take and bake foods as well.

- One Shot Charlie's, 100 W Harrison, 208-689-9968, oneshotcharlies.net, 11-9, hours are seasonal, under $20

  Pizza, hamburgers, sandwiches, salad

## Camping

- Bell Bay Campground, Bell Bay, Hwy. 97 N for 3m, to FR 314 for 3 miles, 6.5m N of Harrison, 877-444-6777, 26 sites, potable water, vault toilets, trail between loops

- Harrison City RV Park, 251 W Harrison St, 208-689-3212, cityofharrison.org

## Lodging

- Corskie House Bed & Breakfast (formerly Wild Boar Inn), 114 N Coeur d'Alene Ave, 208-661-9989, corskiehouse.com, $95, 4 rooms with private baths, full breakfast, wifi

  Rooms are simple and comfortable.

- Lakeview Lodge, 110 N Coeur d'Alene Ave, 208-689-9789, lakeviewlodge-harrison.com, 14 rooms, wifi, $69-285 for 2 bath, 3 bed unit

  A renovated motel with spacious decking, bike parking

- Red Horse Mountain Ranch, 11077 E Blue Lake Rd, Harrison ID, 888-689-9680, redhorsemountain.com, $2000-2700 all inclusive for a week per adult

  All inclusive dude ranch with guided adventures and an extensive kid's program. Adult's only program from late August-Oct. All inclusive packages include horse back riding, archery, fishing, lessons, mountain biking, swimming pool

**Springston** GPS: 47.47N, 116.43W ; Elevation: 2135 ft

*Getting Oriented*

- While there is nothing here anymore, the lumber town that was once Springston is located at the corner of Anderson Lake Rd and E Blue Lake along the Coeur d'Alene River.

*Biking*

- Thomspon Lake Loop, Springston trailhead across the Coeur d'Alene river on Anderson Lake Rd to E Blue Lake Rd Rt to E Thompson lake Rd, left to Hwy. 97 S (left) back to E Blue Lake along the river.

  Trail takes a left out of the trail head and crosses the river intersecting with E Blue Lake Rd where the trail follows the river for a bit and then veers to the left along the S side of Thomspon Lake. Past the lake, take a left on E Thompson Lake Rd where you'll pass the N side of the lake and wind around another smaller body of water and then down to Hwy. 97. A short, 1/2m ride on 97 takes you back to E Blue Lake, left.

- Anderson Lake Loop, Springston trailhead to S Anderson lake Rd to Bell Canyon Rd to Hwy. 97 (Harrison Rd), right and right on Blue Lake Rd back to Springston, 6m long loop

  Trail has one uphill. Trail follows S. Anderson lake Rd right along the lake until it comes to an intersection. Turn rt to E Bell Canyon. At Hwy. 97 turn right for a short ride to E Blue Lake Rd. You'll cross the Coeur d'Alene river but Anderson Lake will be on your right as you return to Springston.

  *Media connection: Friends of the Coeur d'Alene have a nice map of the ride (including where the toilets are), http://friendsofcdatrails.org/maps/for_all/01_AndersonThompsonLakes.pdf*

# Medimont GPS:47.28N, 116.36W ; Elevation: 2182 ft

*Getting Oriented*

- This tiny little town is just N of Cave Lake along S Ruddy Duck Rd but it extends S on S Medimont Rd to Hwy. 3 on the other side of Cave Lake

*Practicalities*

- Grocery

  Valley Mart Grocers, 31504 Hwy. 3, 208-689-3384

*Activities*

- Rainy Hill Boat Launch, on E Rainy Hill Rd, outhouse, boat launch, fishing

*Camping*
- Quiet Nook Campgrounds, 31146 S Hwy 3 MM 104, 208-689-3385, dump station, fire rings, full hookups, cabins, showers, fishing, swimming, hiking

**Lane** GPS: 47.02N, 116.32W ; Elevation: 2169 ft

*Getting Oriented*
- This small town is off Hwy. 3 to the E of the Coeur d'Alene River. Take exit 34 off I90 S.

**Rose Lake** GPS: 47.33N, 116.26W ; Elevation: 2149 ft

*Getting Oriented*

- At Hwy. 3 at S River Rd, just N of the Coeur d'Alene river. Exit 34 off I90

*Dining*
- Rose Lake Restaurant, 11233 S Hwy. 3, gone

- Watson's Resort Historic Bar, 12990 S Hill Drive, 208-682-3604, www.roselakeresort.com, 4-10pm Wed-Thurs, 11-12 Fri-Sun

*Activities*
- Killarney Lake, from I 90, exit 3 5m S to Killarney Lake Rd, 3.5m, fee, drinking water, vault toilets, picnic area, boating, fishing, hiking, hunting

- Rose Lake Boat Launch, hwy 3, restrooms

- Lower Coeur d'Alene River Recreation Area, Hwy. 3 or by boat, 208-769-5000

  Combining 11 lakes and the Coeur d'Alene River, this recreation area is interconnected and includes wetlands.

*Lodging*
- Watson's Rose Lake Resort, 12990 S Hill Drive, Watson Rd, 208-691-0596, www.roselakeresort.com, vacation suite, rustic camping cabins, camping

  Vacation suite has a full kitchen. All units, including rustic cabins, have air con and heat.

**Cataldo** GPS: 47.32N, 116.19W ; Elevation: 2139ft

*Getting Oriented*
- I90 runs to the S of Cataldo, exit 40 off the Interstate. E Canyon Rd/Riverview Rd is the main street.

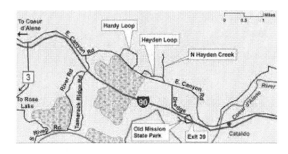

## Map of Cataldo Area
(courtesy of fishandgame.idaho.gov)

*Activities*

- Cataldo Mission, 31732 S Mission Rd, located in the Old Mission State Park, 208-682-3814, see below

  The oldest building in Idaho that is still standing. It was established by the Jesuits in the 1840's. It's construction on its current site was complete in 1853. The mission was completed in Renaissance style using simple tools and untrained labor

- Coeur d'Alene's Old Mission State Park, 31732 S Mission Rd, 208-682-3814, 9-5 seasonally, fee, restrooms

  Includes the Cataldo Mission (see above), the old Parish House and a historic cemetery. Visitor Center on site.

- Peak Adventures, no longer open

- Tamerack Ridge Route, I90 exit 40, turn right onto Latour Creek Rd to the Cataldo Trailhead parking area, 18.7m loop

  Go West on E Canyon Rd to S River Rd/Tamarack Ridge Rd (Stay on Tamarack for a paved but hilly ride or take gravel River), left to River Rd, Rt (packed gravel) to Hwy 3 left, cross the bridge, turn left and continue to Bull Run Trailhead (restroom). Turn left here onto the Trail of the Coeur d'Alenes to the Cataldo Trailhead. Trail is hilly in places and runs along the river for quite a bit.

  *media connection: Friends of the Coeur d'Alene Trail have a nice map of the area, http://friendsofcdatrails.org/maps/for_all/02_TamarackRidge_loop.pdf*

*Dining*

- *The Mission Inn, 36179 E Canyon, 208-682-4435, facebook page updated regularly, 8am-9pm,

Home cooking including large breakfasts with great hashbrowns, pizza, burgers and sandwiches. Salads and house cut fries are good side choices. Known for their huckleberry shakes.

## Camping

- Kahnderosa River Campground, 14343 S Latour Creek Rd, 208-682-4613, drinking water, dump station, full hookups, pull thru sites, showers, on the waterfront, fishing, pets ok

  Park is right off I90 and along the river with lots of shade trees

- Lost Moose Campground, 27706 S Latour Creek Rd, 208-682-3555, www.lostmooserv.com, hookup, cabins, boat launch, fishing, small convenient store

# Hwy. 97 (Lake Coeur d'Alene Scenic Byway)

## Getting Oriented

- Runs S off exit 22 off I90, along Lake Coeur d'Alene to Hwy. 3

## Attractions from N to S

- Wolf Lodge Bay, I 90 exit 22 and turn S at the end of the off ramp to a gravel Rd

- Mullan Trail Road, N at exit ramp, 1/2m to site, 1/2 m interpretive trail

  *Learn More About It: Mullan trail was once a military wagon road back in 1861 directed by Lt John Mullan, a topographical engineer. It was the first civilian engineered road in the Pacific Northwest. The route ran from Fort Walla Walla in Washington to Fort Benton in what is now Montana. The road was well traveled in its day with a mix of miners and pioneers.*

- Blue Creek Bay, I90 to Wolf Lodge Bay exit 22, turn north and follow the Yellowstone Trail Rd for 2m then turn S onto Landing Rd, 208-769-5000, boat launch, fishing, swimming, picnic sites, vault toilet, pet on leash, trail access, good area for Osprey and Bald Eagle siting

- Boat Launch, Wolf Lodge Bay exit 22, S one mile, day use only, fee, boat ramp, vault toilet,

- *Mineral Ridge Scenic Area and National Recreation Trail, exit 22, one mile, fee, picnic area, drinking water, pit toilets, 3.3m trail with interpretive signs

  Gentle uphill climb to the top of the ridge for fantastic views. Bald Eagle area.

- Lake Coeur d'Alene Camping Resort, see under Coeur d'Alene

- Beauty Bay State Recreation Area, Wolf Lodge Bay exit 22 off I90, S on Hwy. 97, picnic area, 1/2m loop trail, viewing deck

- Beauty Creek Campground, 7500 Beauty Creek Rd, Hwy. 97 to FR 438 (Beauty Creek Rd), 208-664-2318, 20 sites, fee, boat ramp, fishing dock, drinking water, canoeing, vault toilets,

    Beauty Creek Overlook Trail, 1.8m trail

    Mt Coeur d'Alene viewpoint trail, 4.9m

    Caribou Ridge National Recreation Trail, 5m moderate climb with outstanding views

- Carlin Bay Resort, 14691 Hwy. 97, 208-689-3295, see listing under Harrison

- Hutton's General Store, see listing under Harrison

## Benewah County

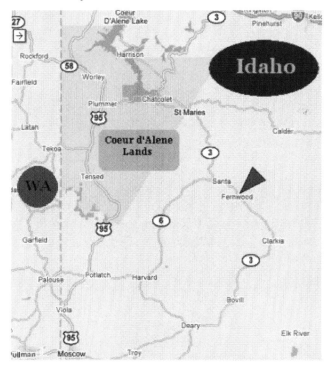

## Map of Benewah County
(Map is Wikimedia Commons in the public domain)

*Getting Oriented*
- On the West side of the county, Hwy. 95 runs North/South and on the East side Hwy. 3 stretches from North to South.

- Named after a Coeur d'Alene tribe, Benewah county abuts Washington State in the panhandle of Idaho. The largest city and county seat is St. Maries with 9200 people.

## Plummer GPS: 47.20N, 115.53 W ; Elevation: 2722 ft.

*Getting Oriented*
- Hwy. 95 runs right through town.

*Practicalities*
- Visitor Information

  www.cityofplummer.org

  Coeur D'Alene Forestry, 208-686-1461, cdatribe-nsn.gov

- Plummer Public Library, 800 Dogwood St, 208-686-1812, plummer.lili.org, 10-6.

*Parks*
- Clark Fisk Park, 880 C St

- Plummer Community Center and Park (Coeur d'Alene Veterans Memorial and Gathering Place), 5th and C St, picnic tables, restrooms, playground, Trail of the Coeur d'Alenes starts here

*Activities*
- Trail of the Coeur d'Alene Recreation Trail, starts at the Community Center, 73m trail that runs from Mullan to Plummer. In Harrison, the trail runs right along the lake. It's a 7m ride/walk south to historic Heyburn State Park, across the causeway and another 10 m to Plummer. This is one of the nicest, most attractive legs of the ride

  *media connection: a brochure is available on line on the Trail*

  *http://www.orrandonneurs.org/sftest/TrailCDAWeb.pdf*

- The Bitterroot Loop, start at the Coeur d'Alene tribal Veteran's memorial park and follow the loop East to Heyburn State Park and North to Harrison then to Cataldo, East to Wallace with a climb to Lookout Pass, then downhill on the Hiawatha trail along the St. Joe River to Avery and then W to St Maries. The last 12m of the route are the most dangerous along a stretch of a local highway with very thin shoulders, 185m of this loop can be done by bike on rail trails and gravel roads. Those who want to avoid any part of the loop can get a shuttle through Hi Water Adventures, 208-582-0177.

*media connection: a local blog is updated regularly on the bitterroot loop at bitterrootloop.wordpress.com. The blog author also has a book, Trail of the Coeur d'Alenes Unofficial Guidebook, Estar Holmes, 2013.*

## Shopping

- Golden Era Antiques, 1624 Long Rd, 208-686-0505, 10-5:30pm, facebook page updated regularly,  picnic tables

  A great assortment of stuff, kitchenware, furniture, jewelry and dresses

## Dining

- Bobbi's Bar, 785 C St, 208-686-1677, local reservation bar

- Gateway Cafe, 126 10th St, 208-686-1314, 6am-7pm

  Fish and chips, sausage, burgers, including buffalo, chicken, homemade soups and pies and a salad bar

- Rising Star Espresso, 1021 D St, 208-686-7277, 6-5pm

- Zips Drive In, 990 D St, 208-686-1331, zipsdrivein.com, chain with burgers, chickens and shakes

## Lodging

- Plummer Motel, 301 10th St, 208-686-1205

## Tensed GPS: 47.9N, 116.55 W ; Elevation: 2562 feet

### Getting Oriented

- Hwy. 95 runs right through town, just one mile N of De Smet (see below).

### Practicalities

- Tensed/De Smet Public Library, 304 C St, 208-274-2922, tensed.lili.org.

### Activities

- DeSmet-Tensed Trail, .85m trail crosses the river, benches, picnic tables

## De Smet GPS: 47.08N, 116.54 W ; Elevation: 2598 feet

### Getting Oriented

- Hwy. 95 runs right through town.

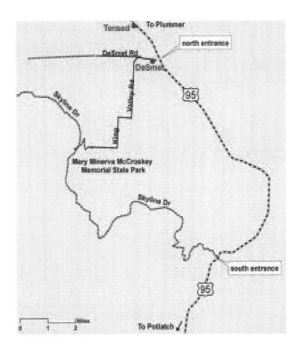

# Map of Mary Minverva McCroskey Memorial Park

(courtesy of fishandgame.idaho.gov)

*Activities*

- DeSmet-Tensed Trail, .85m trail crosses the river, benches, picnic tables

- Mary M McCroskey State Park, from De Smet, take King Valley Rd S to Dole Camp Rd to Skyline Dr, or access Skyline Drive from Hwy. 95, S of De Smet, 208-686-1308, 3000-4300 ft elevation, potable water on Skyline drive, vault toilets, picnic, camping

  Skyline drive, 18 mile unimproved, rough road rises through the 5300 acre park's cedar and ponderosa to look out over the prairies. 32m of multi-purpose trails for horses, mountain bikers, hikers and ATV's are accessible. Huckleberry Mountain and Mission Mountain are 1.5m from the trailheads on Skyline drive.

*Camping*

- Mary M McCroskey State Park, from De Smet, take King Valley Rd S to Dole Camp Rd to Skyline Dr, or access Skyline Drive from Hwy. 95, S of De Smet, 208-686-1308, 3000-4300 ft elevation, 9 sites, potable water on Skyline drive, vault toilets, picnic

- Skyline drive, 18 mile unimproved, rough road rises through the park's cedar and ponderosa to look out over the prairies. 32m of multi-purpose trails for horses, mountain bikers, hikers and ATV's are accessible

*Learn More About it: Mary Minerva McCroskey was once a pioneer woman and her son, Virgil, is the one responsible for this park. He donated the land in 1955 after working hard to acquire the land. Virgil had enjoyed childhood trips to the area and was concerned that logging operations were going to overrun the place. The only way the state would accept the donation was if McCroskey agreed to take care of the land for the first fifteen years, which might not seem like that big a deal, but McCroskey was 79 at the time. He agreed though, and lived long enough to fulfill his part of the deal.*

## Chatcolet Lake Elevation: 2125 feet

### Getting Oriented
- S end of Lake Coeur d'Alene

### Practicalities
- A causeway from the East to the West side of the lake is situated here.

### Activities

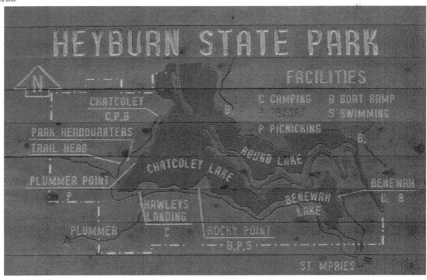

## Map of Heyburn State Park
- *Heyburn State Park, 57 Chatcolet Rd, 208-245-3563, marina, playground, swimming beach, picnic area, camping cabins, restrooms, six trails for a total of 20m, guided walks are offered occasionally from the Coeur d'Alene Audubon society (www.dcaudubon.org).

5744 acres of land and 2300 acres of water. Extensive marshes and shallow lakes provide prime waterfowl habitat. Access to the Trail of Coeur d'Alenes

*media connection: online trail brochure is available,*
*http://www.whitepineinps.org/Annual_Mtg/HSP_Trail_Desc.pdf*

Visitor Center, S side of park, off Hwy. 5 and Chatcolet Rd wifi, interpretive exhibits

Rocky Point Marina, off Chatcolet Rd, rent kayaks, paddleboats, canoes or rowboats, playground, swimming beach, picnic area

Plummer Creek Marsh Interpretive Area, great viewing areas of Marsh, interpretive kiosk explains the migrating birds

## Lodging and Camping

- Heyburn State Park, 208-245-3563, 73 sites, potable water, flush toilets, showers, marina, playground, swimming beach, picnic area, camping cabins, cabins ($50-115), six trails for a total of 20m, guided walks are offered occasionally from the Coeur d'Alene Audubon society (www.dcaudubon.org).

  Cottages have one to two bedrooms, kitchens, air con, but need to bring your own linens.

## Calder GPS: 47.16N, 116.11W ; Elevation: 2185 feet

## Getting Oriented

- On the N side of the St Joe River on Trout Creek Rd.

## Practicalities

- Boise Airport Shuttle, 208-795-7777

  Provides airport transportation to and from Boise Airport.

## Activities

- Big Eddy Marina, 18985 St Joe River Rd, 208-476-5994, restrooms, swim beach, playground, trail head to Freeman Creek

- Pearson to Calder Trail, access in Calder, Marble Creek, Avery and Pearson

  Part of the Idaho Milwaukee Road Rail-Trail system and connects to the Route of the Hiawatha. Calder is the Western most of the towns on this segment.

## Camping

- Huckleberry Campground, Hwy. 50 E from St Maries 29m, 33 units, fee, hookups, dump station, picnic table, fishing, rafting, canoeing, vault toilets,

- St Joe Lodge, Resort and RV Park, MM 33.5 on Hwy. 50, 208-245-3462, 55 sites, Gone?

**St Maries** GPS: 47.316N, 116.57W ; Elevation: 2192 feet

*Getting Oriented*

- At the intersection of Hwy. 3 and Hwy. 5 along the St Joe River. Largest town in the area. Fill up and get your groceries here if you are heading out on Hwy. 50 East.

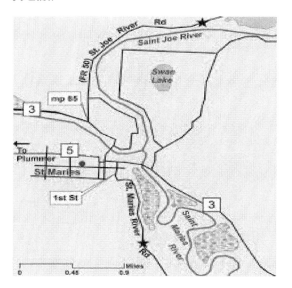

# Map of St Maries
(courtesy of fishandgame.idaho.gov)

*Practicalities*

- Visitor Information

  St Maries Chamber of Commerce, 906 Main, 208-245-3563, stmarieschamber.org

  St Joe Ranger District, 222 7th St, 208-245-2531

- Laundry

  Riverbend Full Services Laundry, 358 S 5th, 208-245-9107

- Library

  St Maries Public Library, 822 W College Ave, 208-245-3732, stmarieslibrary.lili.org

- Grocery

  Archies IGA, 105 E College Ave, 208-245-5504

  Calder General Store, 40 Railroad St, 208-245-5278

  St Maries Harvest Foods, 40 Homer Dr, 208-245-6555, harvestfoodsnw.com

*Parks*

- Aqua Park, 10th St, access to the St Joe River, boat launch, picnic tables, grills, restrooms

- Central park, swimming pool, picnic facilities, playground, dirt track

- Eleanor Park, 11th St and West Idaho Ave,

- Hillcrest Park, Highland Ave and Lincoln Ave

- Loggers Memorial park, Main and 4th,

- Vic Camm Park, 5th St,

- Mullan Trail park, off W Idaho Ave, restrooms

  Turn of the century logging equipment and a steam powered engine

*Activities*

- Cherry Bend Boaters Park, Hwy 3 to Cottonwood Pt Dr, picnic area

- Hughes Home Museum, 538 Main Ave, 208-245-3212, noon-4pm Thurs-Sun.

  History depicted through photos, antiques and artifacts. The house itself was built in 1902 as a men's club, then it became a doctor's office and in 1926 was modernized.

- Murals, downtown

  Selection of vibrant murals are painted throughout the downtown

  *Media Connection, an online brochure explains the murals, http://www.stmarieschamber.org/Mural%20Brochure%20ii.pdf*

- Old Milwaukee Road, accessible at the Marble Creek Interpretive Site, runs between St Maries and Avery along the old railroad bed that follows the St Joe River, biking and hiking

- Round Lake Boat Launch, from Hwy 97, turn SE on O'Gara Rd to S Benewah Rd, fishing, restrooms

- St Joe Outfitters and Guides, 8311 Windfall Pass Rd, 208-245-4002, www.stjoeoutfitters.com, fly fishing and guided pack trips

- White Pine Scenic Drive, from St Maries, take Hwy. 3/6 South to Potlatch (Hwy. 3 also travels N to I90)

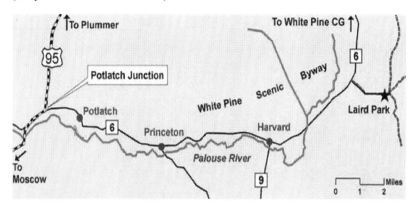

## Map of White Pine Scenic Drive
(courtesy of fishandgame.idaho.gov)

Paved road is mixture of farmlands, forests, rivers and mountains and the Palouse Prairie, a series of rolling hills.

Palouse Divide, Hwy. 6 to North South Ski Area, 9m of marked hiking and nordic ski trails and 25m of backcountry trails, starting at 3600ft. Trails are accessed from both sides of the highway, though the East side has more groomed trails.

Giant White Pine Campground, 14 sites, drinking water, fee, largest stand of White Pines in North America and excellent birding here, 3m loop hiking trail with a couple of longer hiking options available as well

Laird Park, 31 sites, camping, vault toilets, swimming with sandy beach, rock hounding, 1/2m interpretive trail, picnic tables set among pine and cedar trees

Harvard, see separate listing

Princeton, see separate listing

- Woodlawn Cemetery and Firefighters' Circle, Hwy. 5, W of St Maries

Cemetery includes the graves of 57 firefighters killed in the 1910 fire.

*Dining*

- Bud's Drive In, 101 W College Ave, 208-245-3312, facebook page updated regularly, 4am-8pm, drive in, indoor and outdoor eating

  Burger, fries, ice cream, and a basic, American breakfast menu. Check the facebook page for dinner specials

- Cabin City Pizza, 2242 W Idaho Ave, 208-245-2561, facebook page updated regularly, 11am-7pm

  Pizza, salad and seafood. Frequent dinner specials are listed on facebook

- Casa de Oro Family Mexican Restaurant, 900 Golf Course Rd, 208-245-3200, 11am-10pm, full bar, wifi

  Traditional Mexican offerings. Golf course views with occasional deer or elk sightings.

- Grub Box, 201 N 8th St, 208-245-8205, facebook page updated with specials, 9:30-5:30, under $10, inside seating

  Soup and sandwiches, burgers and fries

- Handi Corner, 929 Main, 208-245-3400, facebook page, 4:30am-9pm

  Traditional American breakfasts and burgers and fries the rest of the day

- Hill A Beans, Railroad Ave, 208-245-5539

- Julian Java, 132 N 1st St, 208-245-4960, 6:30-3:30pm, drive through

  Seattle's best coffee and fruit freezes

- Junction Drive In, 213 W College Ave, 208-245-3416, drive in and inside eating

  Old fashioned drive in with burgers, fries and shakes and some Mexican choices

- Los Mexicana's Taco Shack, Homer Dr, 208-582-4293, 11am-7pm

  Burritos and tacos

- Main Street Antiques & Espresso, 806 Main Ave, 208-245-5539, facebook page,

- Pizza Factory, 910 Main Ave, 208-245-5515, pizzafactory.com, wifi

Hand tossed pizza in the traditional style

- Sally's Handi Corner Family Dining, 929 Main Ave, 208-245-3400

  Full breakfast anytime

- Zip's Drive In, 127 E College Ave, 208-245-1700

  chain burgers

*Camping*
- Scott Park, 14m E of St Maries at MP 14, fire pit, picnic area, boat lanch, vault toilet, no drinking water

- Shady River RV Park, 84752 Hwy. 3, 208-245-3549

- St Maries Misty Meadows RV Park & Campground, 2800 St Joe River Rd, 208-245-2639, full hookups, on the river

*Lodging*
- Birch Tree bed & Breakfast, 1 Jay Lane, 208-245-2198, not sure it's still there

- Fort Hemenway Manor B & B, 1001 Jefferson Ave, 208-245-7979, www.forthemenwaymanor.com, $85-275, full gourmet breakfast, wifi

  Located above St Maries on a hill with a large front porch. Rooms vary widely from elaborate plush red decor to simple white cast iron. Living room and porch for guest use.

- The Pines Motel, 1117 Main Ave, 208-245-2545, www.stmariesmotel.com, basic motel

- Ponderosa Lane Bed & Breakfast, 30 Ponderosa Ln, 208-245-6639, ponderosalanebb.comSt Joe Riverfront bed and breakfast, 816 Shepherd Rd, 208-245-8687, www.stjoeriverbb.com, private and shared bath, $80-140 with full breakfast, wifi

  Small, simple rooms with Americana decor including quilts on the beds. Common spaces include a patio and fire pit.

- River Front Suites, 105 Main Ave, 208-582-1724, www.riverfrontsuites.com, 5 one-two bedroom units with river views, kitchens, $85-100

  Units are simple and comfortable

- Rio Mirada Ranch B & B, 3717 St Maries River Rd, 3.7m from St Maries, 208-245-3276, continental breakfast or full country breakfast, $125

  Guests stay in an apartment onsite with two bedrooms

- St Joe Riverfront B & B, 816 Shepherd Rd, 208-245-8687, www.stjoeriverbb.com, four rooms with private and shared baths, $139-139

  Contemporary home with lots of decks and views of the area including wildlife and the river.

## Emida GPS: 47.116N, 116.59 W ; Elevation: 2850 ft

*Getting Oriented*
- Off Hwy. 6

*Dining*
- *Drifters Western Bar and Grill, 28554 Hwy. 6, 208-245-1301, facebook page updated regularly, 7am-9pm

  Basically, Drifters is Emida. The roadhouse is a full service eatery and neighborhood hang out. Burgers, green chile, big breakfasts. This place is worth a stop.

## Santa GPS: 47.09N, 116.26 W ; Elevation: 2661 ft

*Getting Oriented*
- Off Hwy. 3

*Practicalities*
- Not much here

## Fernwood GPS: 47.06N, 116.23W ; Elevation: 2733 ft

*Getting Oriented*
- Off hwy. 3

*Practicalities*
- Grocery

  Fernwood Mercantile, 64147 Hwy. 3, 208-245-2098

- Restrooms

  Tri Community Library, 46 Isaacson, 208-245-4883

*Dining*

- Cookies Chuck Wagon, 64019 Hwy. 3, 208-245-4196, 12-10pm

  Large portions, salad bar, American food.

## Shoshone County

*Getting Oriented*

- Shoshone County is located in the Northeast side of the panhandle abutting Montana. There are seven incorporated cities, most of which lie along I90. This corridor is also known as the Silver Valley because of its mineral history

- Website: www.shoshonecounty.org

### Kingston GPS: 47.32N, 116.16 W ; Elevation: 2169 feet

*Getting Oriented*

- Just S of I90. Coeur d'Alene River Rd heads North.

*Dining*

- The Snake Pit, closed

*Camping and Lodging*

- Albert's Landing River Resort, 418 Old River Rd, 208-682-4179, www.albertslanding.com, RV sites, river access, general store, tube rental, shuttle available, fishing

- Bumbleebee Campground, FR 9 for 5 miles then FR 209 for 3, 25 sites, potable water, vault toilets

- Country Lane Inn & RV Resort on the River, 5927A Old River Rd, 208-682-2698, www.countrylaneresort.com, 37 sites, bed and breakfast, bunkhouse, pool/spa, pets allowed

  Heads up: This place gets really critical reviews, so check it out before you reserve.

### Pinehurst GPS: 47.32N, 116.14 W ; Elevation 2224ft

*Getting Oriented*

- Just S of I90 at exit 45.

*Practicalities*

- Grocery

  Barneys, 117 N Division, 208-682-2621

- Laundry

  Laundry xpress, 608 N Division St, 208-682-3212

- Restrooms

  Pinehurst Kingston library, 107 Main St, 208-682-3483

*Activities*
- West Shoshone Park, exit 45 to N. Division, restroom

*Dining*
- Brewed Awakening, 802 N Division St, 208-682-2248, 6am-5pm, serves Silver Cup Coffee

- Tall Pine Drive In, 203 N Division Ave, 208-682-4294, facebook page updated regularly with specials, 11am-7pm, under $10

  Sandwiches, soup, fish and chips and ice cream

*Camping*
- By the Way Campground, 907 N Division, 208-682-3311, bythewaycampground.com, 15 sites, small cabin, hookups, dump station, bathrooms, showers, picnic tables

# Smelterville GPS: 47.32N, 116.10W ; Elevation: 2234 ft

*Getting Oriented*
- I 90 at exit 48

*Practicalities*
- Visitor Information

  Coeur d'Alene River Ranger Station, 173 Commerce Dr, 208-783-2363

- Grocery

  Walmart, 583 Commerce Dr, 208-783-2739

  Wayside Market, 217 Main St, 208-786-9321

*Activities*
- Trail of the Coeur d'Alene comes through town, just N of Main St.

*Dining*
- Espresso Barn, 100 E Main, 208-786-0905, facebook page, 6am-4pm, drive thru

**Wardner** GPS: 47.31N, 116.8W ; Elevation: 2657 ft

**Kellogg** GPS: 47.32N, 116.7 W ;  Elevation: 2303 ft

*Getting Oriented*
- I 90 runs through the center of Kellogg with downtown S of the interstate. S Division is the main N/S road.

*Practicalities*
- Visitor Center

  Historic Silver Valley Chamber of Commerce, 10 Station Ave, 208-784-0821

- Grocery

  Yokes Fresh Market, 117 N Hill, 208-783-1171, 6:30-10, full service grocery

- Laundry

  Laundry Express, 97 Riverside Ave E, 208-783-0702

- Library

  City of Kellogg Library, 16 W Market, 208-787-7231

*Biking*
- Excelsior Cycle, 21 Railroad, 208-786-3751, rental bikes

- Silver Mountain Resort, 610 Bunker Ave, 866-344-2675, www.silvermt.com,bike rentals, take the Gondola to the top of the mountain and ride down

- Kellogg Silverton Loop, I90 to exit 51, turn S on Division St and turn right in the Kellogg Depot Trailhead of the Trail of the Coeur d'Alenes. Riders can go all the way to Silverton (18.5 RT) or a variety of shorter rides, Elizabeth Park (3.25m), Big Creek Loop (7.75m), Gene Day Park loop (11m).

  *Media Connection: friends of the Coeur d'Alenes have a map of this route, http://friendsofcdatrails.org/maps/for_all/11_SilverValleyRoad_loops.pdf*

*Activities*
- Bunker Hill Mine Museum, 140 Railroad Ave, 208-783-1101,

- Crystal Gold Mine, 51931 Silver Valley Rd, 208-783-4653, www.goldmine-idaho.com,

1880's underground gold mine with daily tours from Feb -Dec. 10-4pm winter, 9-6pm summer, $12 adult

- The Gondola at Silver Mountain, exit 45 I90 to Silver Mountain base village, $17 adult, family $54.

  The Gondola is the longest in the world and runs 3.1miles up 3400 ft with views into Canada.

- Kellogg City Park & Swimming Pool, N Hill St,

- Shoshone County Mining and Smelting Museum/Bunker Hill Staff House Museum, 820 McKinley Ave, 208-786-4141, staffhousemuseum.com, 10-6pm, closed Tues, seasonal

  The history of mining is explored in this three story museum. Also some outside exhibits.

- Silver Mountain Resort, 610 Bunker Ave, 866-344-2675, www.silvermt.com, skiing, indoor waterpark, gondola rides, rafting and water sports, mountain biking

- Trail of the Coeur d'Alene runs along W Station Ave.

*Dining*
- Casa De Oro, 120 W Cameron Ave, 208-784-1360, 11am-10pm

  Lively Mexican restaurant with the usual Mexican selections, mole and even burgers.

- Broken Wheel Restaurant, 102 E Cameron Ave, 208-784-0601

  Steak, fish, salad bar

- Hill Street Depot, 446 Railroad Ave, 208-512-4517, facebook page updated with weekly specials, 11-9pm, indoor and outdoor seating

  Full service restaurant in a small home with sandwiches, soup and excellent desserts. Beer on tap and tvs. Smoke their own meats on site.

- Humdinger Drive In, 205 N Hill St, 208-786-7395, outside seating

  Hamburgers, ice cream, tater tots

- Jolt N Bolt, 203 W Cameron Ave, 208-512-2502

- Moose Creek Grill, 12 Emerson Ln, 208-783-2625, www.moosecreekgrill.com, exit 51, under $25

  Set in a large old home with a wide front porch, the family friendly restaurant offers casual comfort. Menu isn't large and focuses on flavorful preparations of fish, pork and chicken. A lighter menu also includes salads, burgers and wraps

- My Big Fat Greek Deli, 110N Hill St, 208-784-1166, www.bigfatgreekdeli.com, website doesn't work, maybe closed?

- Mogul's Lounge, 610 Bunker Ave, 208-783-1111

  Burgers, fish and appetizers

- Mountain Cafe, in Silver Mountain Gondola Village, 610 Bunker Ave, 208-783-0562, mountaincafeandcatering.com, 7:30-12, until 5pm on Sat, closed Tues-Weds., under $10

  Housemade traditional American breakfast, coffee, espresso drinks and sandwiches and salad for lunch.

- Noah's Canteen, 610 Bunker Ave, 208-783-2440

- Sam's, 711 W Cameron Ave, 208-783-0520

  Old fashioned favorites like Chicken Fried Steak, full American breakfasts

- Silver Cup Coffee Roasters, 135 E Cameron Ave, 208-784-3164 , www.silvercupcoffeeroasters.com, Tues, Thurs, Sat.

- The Pizza Palace, 315 McKinley Ave W, 208-783-1323, facebook page updated regularly, 9am-8pm, delivery, under $20

- Wah Hing Restaurant, 215 McKinley Ave, 208-873-3181, Chinese food

- Wildcat Pizza, Gondola Village, 610 Bunker Ave, 208-784-1957, under $20, delivery, 11am-9pm, until 11pm on Fri/Sat

  Slices and full pizzas, salad and wings

## Camping
- Crystal Gold Mine & RV Park, 51931 Silver Valley Rd, 208-783-4653, RV full hook ups, pets welcome

## Lodging
- Emerson Courtyard, 18 Emerson Lane, 208-512-0092

- Guesthouse Inn and Suites, 601 Bunker Ave, 208-783-1234, chain

- Silverhorn Motor Inn, 699 W Cameron Ave, 208-783-1151, website doesn't work, very old motel

- Silver Mountain Morning Star Lodge, 602 Bunker Ave, 208-783-0202, www.silvermt.com, hot tub, water park, fire pits, tennis courts, cafe on site, snowboarding, wifi, access to water park, $199-359

## Osburn GPS: 47.30N, 116.0 W ; Elevation: 2520 ft.

### Getting Oriented

- I90 runs to the East of town, exit at 57. Mullan Ave is the main street through town.

### Practicalities

- Restrooms

  Osburn Library, 921 Mullan Ave, 208-752-9711, osburn.lili.org

- Parks

  Gene Day Park, I90, exit 57 toward Osburn and turn Right onto E Mullan as it turns into Yellowstone Ave to Johnston St/Terror Gulch Rd turn left, restrooms

- Grocery

  Stein's Market, 712 E Mullan Ave, 208-752-5021

### Activities

- Trail of the Coeur d'Alene goes through town

### Camping

- Blue Anchor RV Park, 300 W Mullan, 208-752-3443, www.blueanchorrv.com, wifi, full hookups, pullthrus, showers, laundry, pets welcome

  Shady sites but pretty close together. The park borders I90

### Lodging

- Idaho vacation apartments, 327 W Mullan Ave, 208-753-4111, www.idahovacationapartments.com, wifi, pet friendly, kitchenettes,

## Silverton GPS: 47.29N, 115.57W ; Elevation: 2728 ft

### Getting Oriented

- Silverton is just N of I90 at exit 60. The main road through town is Markwell Ave

### Practicalities

- Parks

Silverton park, off W Yellowstone Ave.

## Wallace GPS: 47.28N, 115.55 W ; Elevation: 2730 ft

### Getting Oriented

- Wallace is a step back in town given that the entire town is on the National Register of Historic Places. It has the feel of a turn of the century mining camp. In an area of Idaho where many towns are economically strapped, Wallace is one of the more attractive places for tourists.

- Just south of I90 at exit 61.

*Did you know? 1.2 billion ounces of silver were mined in this area since mining started in 1884*

### Practicalities

- Visitor Information

Historic Wallace Chamber of Commerce, 10 River St, I90 exit 61, 800-434-4204, wallaceidahochamber.com

- Library

Wallace Public Library, 415 River St, 208-752-4571, noon-8pm, closed Sat-Sun

Restored Carnegie Library, built in 1911.

- Laundry

Sam Brooks Wallace Laundromat, 521 Cedar St, 208-753-7061

- Grocery

Harvest Foods, 800 Bank St, 208-752-1233

### Events

- Wallace Blues Festival, July

### Culture and History

- Mine Heritage Exhibit, 10 River St, exit 61, outside exhibit at the visitor center

- Oasis Bordello Museum, 605 Cedar St, 208-753-0801, $5, 10-5, seasonal

  The hotel was in business of one kind or another until 1988. Today, a tour explains the history of the building and its bawdy past, left as it was in 1988. If nothing else, the plain decor and working girl emphasis is a reminder that TV is not the best portrayal of the "real thing". Murals and a gift shop are also on site.

  *Kid Alert: Is this a museum for kids? Well . . . depends on just how much information on a brothel you want the kiddies to have. The museum is not explicit visually, however.*

  *Did you know? Until 1973, there were five brothels operating in Wallace, none were legal but local police had taken a hands-off approach since the town was established in 1884. However, the Federal authorities intervened, finally, forcing locals to shut down the industry.*

- Northern Pacific Railroad Depot Museum, 219 6th St, 208-752-0111, www.npdepot.org,

  The two story museum is set in a turn of the 19th century building.

- Sierra Silver Mine Tour, 420 5th St, 208-752-5151, www.silverminetour.org, May 1st-Oct 6, 10-4pm tours on the 1/2 hour, $14 adult, $45 for a family

  The mine temp is a moderate 50 degrees. Tours travel on a 16 passenger vintage trolley with a retired miner who provides commentary of current and historic mining history

- Sixth Street Melodrama, 212 6th St, 208-752-8871, www.sixthstreetmelodrama.com

  Set in an 1891 building, the Lux theater seats 80 people and showcases a variety of melodramas and variety shows

- Wallace District Mining Museum, 509 Bank St, 208-556-1592, wallaceminingmuseum.org, 9-5, seasonal,

  Mining history with artifacts and exhibits. An 18 minute video highlights the gold and silver rushes and the great fire of 1910.

*Hiking*
- Pulaski Tunnel/Trail, exit 61 toward I90 Bus/Wallace and stay on I90 Business route (Route 10) to 2nd St, Rt. Follow 2nd street to Bank Street and turn right. Bank street turns into King street turns into Placer Creek Rd/National Forest Rd 456/Moon Pass Rd for one mile, vault toilets, 4m RT hiking only

  Interpretive signs explain the Nicholson mine/Pulaski Tunnel history where Edward Pulaski led his crew during the 1910 fire.

*Learn More About it: The 1910 fire wrecked devastation on the Idaho National Forest, burning 3 million acres of forest and resulting in the death of 78 fire fighters. Drought and train sparks started the fire and Ranger Ed Pulaski was the crew chief of one of the fire crews sent to put it out or contain it. When the fire soared close, Pulaski led his men into an old mine tunnel saving 39 out of his 45 man crew. It was this fire that started the forest service policy of total fire suppression, a practice that lasted for decades. It's only been in the last 20 years or so that the forest service has been shifting its view to a combination of controlled burn and suppression.*

*Media Connection: Download a short brochure on the trail, http://www.fs.usda.gov/Internet/FSE_DOCUMENTS/stelprdb5444702.pdf*

*Year of the Fires: The Story of the Great Fires of 1910, Stephen Pyne, 2008, tells the story of the 1910 fires.*

## Outdoor Activities

- Silver Streak Zipline Tours, 516 Pine St, 208-556-1690, silverstreakziplinetours.com, reservations required, seasonal, $90 per course about 2 hours, weight limits are 85lbs-270lbs

  3 miles of cable soar above the Silver Valley in a two course set up (cost is for ONE course).

- Lookout Pass Ski Area, I90 exit 0, 208-744-1301, skilookout.com, 9am-4pm, food court and pub, $39 full day for adult, ski rentals of skis, boots and poles, options for all ages

- Trail of the Coeur d"Alenes runs through town

## Shopping

- Placer Village Books, 600 Cedar St, at Tabor's Emporium, 208-556-2821, new and used books

## Wine, Beer and Cocktails

- City Limits Pub at North Idaho Mountain Brewery, 108 Nine Mile Rd, 208-556-1120,

  Burgers, nachos and fish and chips

## Dining

- 1313 Club, 608 Bank St, 208-752-9391, www.1313club.com/frontend/cgi-bin/bulletin.cgi, all day dining, full bar, almost everything is under $15

  Mexican, sandwiches, burgers, pasta and steak. Traditional breakfast but also a few Mexican options.

- Angie's on Bank St, 5171/2 Bank St, 208-556-1444, wallace-id.com/ej.html,

Gourmet subs, ice cream, pizza, fudge, espresso

- The Brooks Restaurant, 500 Cedar St, 208-752-8171, www.thebrookshotel.com,

  Full breakfasts including Huckleberry pancakes, American diner food

- City Limits Pub and Grill, 108 Nine Mile Rd, 208-556-1885, citylimitspubandgrill.com, under$20

  On site brewery makes for a great glass of beer with your meal of burgers, wings, salad, steak or pasta. Very eclectic menu.

- Fainting Goat: A Wine Bar and eatery, 516 Bank St, 208-556-1650, faintinggoatwinebar.com, 11:30-close, under $10

  Small plates with salads, tacos, charcuterie and chili,

- Farm Girls Tea Shoppe, 518 Bank St, 208-556-1386, facebook page, 9am-5:30

- The Nook, 519 1/2 Cedar

  Sandwich shop.

- Pizza Factory, 612 Bank St, 208-753-9003, wallace.pizzafactory.com, 11am-8pm, delivery, under $20

  Think and thick crust pizza with the usual toppings, salad, subs including meatball and bbq chicken, and pasta

- Red Light Garage, 302 5th St, 208-556-0575, www.redlightgarage.com, food all day, full bar

  Known for their huckleberry shakes, The Red Light also tacos, burgers and American breakfasts.

- Silver Corner Bar and Grill, 601 Cedar, 208-753-4261, still here?

- The Silver Tea Room, 618 Bank St, 208-556-1500, www.pricetagantiques.com,

  Full tea service with lunch sandwiches and cookies inside an antique store.

- Smoke House BBQ and Saloon, 424 6th St, 208-659-7539, www.smokehousebbqsaloon.com, 11:30-10pm, almost everything is under $20

  Pull pork, brisket and the usual BBQ but also some not so usual like a bison burger, potato chips topped with BBQ sauce. Old fashioned atmosphere but also no air conditioning

*Camping*

- Wallace RV Park, 108 Nine Mile Rd, 208-753-7121, wallacervpark.com, 35 sites, dry cabins with no linens, pull thru, restrooms, showers, wifi

  Sites are small and do NOT include picnic table or fire pit.

*Lodging*

- The Beale House, 107 Cedar St, 208-752-7151, wallace-id.com/bealehouse.html, $225, 5 rooms, full breakfast

  Bed and breakfast

- The Brooks Hotel, 500 Cedar St, 208-752-8171, www.thebrookshotel.com, rooms and suites, wifi

  Older hotel with basic amenities.

- Hercules Inn, 208-556-0575, redlightgarage.com/hercules-inn/, 4 suites, wifi, laundry, hot tub, $75

- Ryan Hotel, 608 Cedar St, 208-753-6001, wallace-id.com/ryan_hotel.html,

  Building was built in 1903, once a residential hotel, now a tourist stop. Rooms have period decor.

- Stardust Motel, 410 Pine St, 208-752-1213, stardustmotelidaho.com

  The stardust motel's sign seems to date from the vibrant 50's, but the motel appears to be more recently renovated. Basic motel rooms

- Wallace Inn, 100 Front St, 800-643-2386, wallaceinn.com, website doesn't work

# Woodland Park  GPS: 48.23 N, 114.27 W ; Elevation: 3205 ft

*Getting Oriented*

- Off hwy. 4, N of I90 Nothing here.

# Prichard  GPS: 47.41N, 115.55W ; Elevation: 2405ft

*Getting Oriented*

- On Coeur d'Alene River Rd

*Activities*

- Avery Creek Picnic Area, 4m N of Prichard on paved FR 208, vault toilets, potable water, picnic units, short trail, fishing

- Prichard Bridge, 1m S of Prichard on paved FR 208, vault toilets, picnic area

*Dining*
- Prichard Tavern, 183 Prichard St, 208-682-2944, 10am-12am

*Camping*
- Berlin Flat Campground, 5m N on FR 208 then 9m on FR 412 (all paved but two miles), potable water, vault toilets

- Big Hank Campground, FR 208 20 miles, 6 sites, potable water, vault toilets

- Devil's Elbow Campground, FR 208 14m, 20 sites, potable water, vault toilets

- Kit Price Campground, FR 208 11 miles, vault toilets, potable water,

## Murray GPS: 47.37N, 115.51W W; Elevation: 2785 ft

*Getting Oriented*
- Off Thompson Pass Rd (Forest Rd 9)

*Activities*
- Sprag pole Museum, 6353 Prichard Creek Rd, 208-682-3901, free

  9000 sq ft museum filled with mining stuff (filled!)

*Dining*
- Spragpole Museum-Bar-Cafe, 6353 Prichard Creek Rd, 208-682-3901,

  Ribs, burgers, fish and chips, soup, huge servings

## Mullan; GPS: 47.28N, 115.47 W; Elevation: 3278 feet

*Getting Oriented*
- Off I 90 at exit 68-69.

*Practicalities*
- Mullan Public Library, 117 Hunter St, 208-744-1220, mullan.lili.org

*Activities*
- Captain John Mullan Museum, 229 Earle St, 208-744-1717, mullanmuseum.org, 10-4 seasonal, free, restrooms

  Historical exhibits on Mullan history are displayed in an old theater built in 1915

- NorPac Trail, exit 68, park along River St between 2nd and 3rd

Trail runs from Mullan at the trailhead for the Trail of the Coeur d'Alenes to Saltese, paved for the first 4 miles. At 20 miles it intersects the Route of the Hiawatha

- Shoshone Park, I 90 exit 68 or 69, 3m E of Mullan on S. Fork Coeur D'Alene rd (Larson Rd), 21 sites, 877-444-6777, potable water, restrooms, interpretive sign, fish hatchery, historic cabin

- Stevens Lakes, Take exit 69 from I90 and head towards Mullan, turning Rt onto Friday ave/Willow Creek Rd to the end where the trail starts, 2m one way, 1800 ft elevation change

    Trail climbs swiftly up to an Alpine Lake and to the Idaho/Montana border.

*Dining*
- Breanda's Bitterroot Coffee House, 235 Hunter St, 208-512-0813, facebook updated regularly, 7am-3pm

    Coffee, sandwiches, quesadillas, sweets

- Earle's Pub & Grub, 206 Earle Ave, 208-744-1700, facebook page, 2pm-11am

    Chicken fried steak, burgers in large portions

- Outlaw Bar, 209 Hunter Ave, 208-744-1120

*Camping*
- Shoshone Park, I 90 exit 68 or 69, 3m E of Mullan on S. Fork Coeur D'Alene rd (Larson Rd), 21 sites, 877-444-6777, potable water, restrooms, interpretive sign, fish hatchery, historic cabin

*Lodging*
- Mullan House Bed and Breakfast, for sale

**Avery** GPS: 47.15N, 115.48W ; Elevation: 2486 ft

*Getting Oriented*
- Avery, road is paved, Hwy. 50; 47m from St Maries and another 42m to the Montana border. Avery seems to be a town on its last leg with a rash of fires burning down public buildings and few services left. But, the area has great fishing and hiking.

*Practicalities*
- Visitor Information

Red Ives Information Center, 29m E of Avery on St Joe Rd (Hwy. 50), vault toilets,

Avery Ranger Station, from Hwy. 50, take Dunn Peak Rd (FR 1934)

- Grocery

Scheffy's General Store, 95 Milwaukee Rd, 208-245-4410, scheffys.com, for sale but open, deli sandwiches and full line of groceries, laundry

Avery Trading Post, 214 Avery, 208-245-3996, burned down

*Activities*

- Fish Lake and Lost Lake Trail, FR 301 S for 13m, then FR 216 E for one mile to FR 1925 for 2m S, elevation from 4920-5460, Fish Lake is 2m one way; Lost Lake is 2.7m one way

- Marble Creek Interpretive Site, Hwy. 50 E and 6m N on FR 321, 3000 ft elevation, picnic area, fishing, restrooms

  Interpretive panels explain how loggers transported the white pine from the nearby forests

- Upper St Joe River Trail, 17m trail

- Upper Landing Picnic Area, 1m East of Avery on Hwy. 50, vault toilets, picnic sites, potable water, fishing, access to Nelson Ridge Trail

- Historic Avery Ranger Station, Dunn Peak Rd (FR 1934) E and then N through town for .3m

  Ranger station was started in 1909 and finally completed in 1936. It is still in use, but several historic buildings remain on the property. And visitors can view the buildings from outside.

*Camping*

- Line Creek Stock Camp, S on Red Ives Rd (FR 218) 11 m, 11 sites, no water, vault toilets, fishing, St Joe River Trailhead access

- Spruce Tree Campground, Red Ives Rd #218, 9 sites, potable water, vault toilets, fishing, access to St Joe River Trail #48

- Telichpah Campground, 6m N of Avery on St Joe Rd (#456), turn S for 1m on Old Moon Pass Rd, 5 sites, vault toilets, access to Nelson Peak National Recreation Trail

- Turner Flat Campground, 8m E of Avery, 11 sites, drinking water, vault toilets, fishing, fee

*Lodging*

- Avery Gift Shop Lodging, 61 Old River Rd, 208-245-1303, basic room above a gift shop

- Scheffy's Motel, 95 Milwaukee Rd, 208-245-4410, scheffys.com, air con, for sale but open

  Basic motel

- Swiftwater Lodge/Cabins by the Joe, 730 Siberts Old River Rd, 425-773-3724, cabinsbythejoe.com, picnic area, fire pit, kitchenette. RV sites have full hookup, fishing,

  Small cabins with wood trim and comfy quilts and RV sites along the river

# Clarkia GPS 47.00N, 116.15 W; elevation: 862ft

*Getting Oriented*

- Clarkia is off Hwy. 3.

# Map of Clarkia

(From Wikipedia with open commons license)

*Practicalities*

- Library

  Clarkia Free Library District, 377 Poplar St, 208-245-2908

*Activities*

- Delaney Creek National Recreation Trail (#273), 26m E of Clarkia on Forest Rd 301, July-Sept, elevation from 4400-6400ft, 4.25m one way, access to 45 miles of trails in the Marble Creek System in Grandmother Mountain Wilderness Study Area

Trail goes past cabin remains, logging camps, fishing and huckleberry bushes

- Hobo Cedar Grove Botanical Area (#255), FR 321 NE from Clarkia to FR 3357

  .5m interpretive trail through 240 acre ancient cedar grove of 500 year old cedars that were bypassed by the extensive logging of the surrounding forest. A one mile loop trail is also available.

- Emerald Creek Campground, FR 447 6m, 18 sites, potable water, vault toilet, fishing, picnic area

- Emerald Creek Garnet, Hwy. 3 S for 24m to FR 447 8m, 9am-5pm Fri-Tues Memorial Day-Labor Day, picnic tables, restrooms, fee

  1/2m trail to the sluice area where the unique gems might be found. There are only two places in the world with star garnets. The other is in India.

  *media connection: for detailed information about the garnet site, see http://www.stmarieschamber.org/garnet.html*

- Clarkia Fossil beds, 2m S of Clarkia on Hwy. 3, fee, the fossil beds are on private property

  *Learn More About It: The area around Clarkia was once a prehistoric lake. 15 million years ago silt accumulated at the bottom of the lake making the perfect medium for preserving plant and fish fossils. Without air, the fish and plants decomposed slowly allowing for preservation of the soft tissues, the lines and marks you see in the fossils.*

- Fossil Bowl Racing, 52450 Hwy 3, 208-245-3608, www.fossilbowl.com, motocross track and off-road trails

- Grandmother Mountain Recreation Area, 10m E on FR 301

  12,000 acre recreation area. There are four moderate loop trails that pass through meadows and forests and fishing holes. All terrain vehicles are allowed here as well.

*Camping*
- Cedar Creek Campground, 3m N of Hwy. 3, 3 sites, picnic sites, vault toilet, no water, fee

# Latah County

*Getting Oriented*

- Latah county is on the Idaho and Washington border in an area known as "The Palouse", a kind of bread basket of the border. Both University of Idaho and Washington State University are in the Palouse. Moscow is the largest town in Latah County.

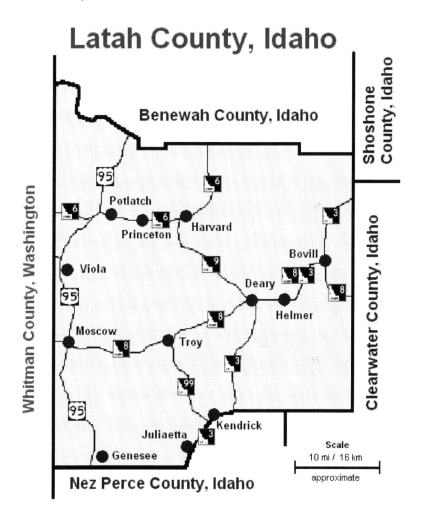

## Map of Nez Perce County

(From Wikimedia Commons, released into the public domain)

*Activities*

- Latah Trail, currently under construction but will eventually run from Moscow Idaho to Troy, providing a 22 mile non-motorized trail, connecting to the Paradise path in Moscow, the Chipman Trail between Moscow and Pullman and the Ed Corkill Memorial River Trail between kendrick and Juliaetta.

*Media Connection: See information about the Latah Trail at the Latah Trail Foundation, http://www.latahtrailfoundation.org/maps/*

## Moscow GPS: 46.43N, 116.59 W ; Elevation: 2579 ft

### Getting Oriented

- On the West edge of Idaho, Moscow is the home of Idaho State University. Hwy. 95 runs N/S through the city. The University of Idaho is just W of Hwy. 95. Hwy. 8 runs along the N edge of the campus.

### Practicalities

- Visitor Information

  Moscow Chamber of Commerce, 411 S Main St, www.moscowchamber.com, 9am-5pm

- Library

  Latah County Library District, 110 S Jefferson St, 208-882-3925, 10-6pm

- Grocery

  Moscow Food Co-op, 121 E 5th St, 208-882-8357, moscowfood.coop, 7:30-9pm

  Phung Market, 317 W 6th St, 208-892-0938

  Rosauers Supermarkets, 411 N Main St, 208-882-5574

  Safeway, 1320 S Blaine St, 208-883-0713

  Walmart Supercenter, 2470 W Pullman Rd, 208-883-8828

### Events

- Rendezvous in the Park, July music festival, 208-882-1178

- The Lionel Hampton Jazz Festival, Feb, 208-885-6231

### Shopping

- Bookpeople of Moscow, 521 S Main St, 208-882-7957, 10-8pm

  Independent, locally owned bookstore

### Parks

- Almon Asbury Lieuallen Park, 500 Residence St, playground, picnic area

- Alturas Park, 1241 Alturas Dr, picnic area, gardens

- Anderson Frontier Park, 890 West Palouse River Dr, playground, picnic area, wetland and small pond

- Berman Creekside Park, 382 Styner Ave, picnic area, sledding hill

- Dog Park, 2019 White Ave, 1 acre fenced area

- East City Park, 900 East Third St, playground, restrooms, summer concerts on Thursday evening

- East Gate Park, 1200 Kamiaken St, play area, picnic area, playground

- Ghormley Park, 504 Home St, play area, picnic shelter, playground, restrooms

- Heron's Hideout Park, 1200 South Mountain View Rd, observation deck, creek restoration area

- Jim Lyle Rotary Park, 1100 F St, play area, picnic area, restrooms

- Kiwanis Park, 2027 E St, restrooms, picnic shelter, pond, fishing

- Lena Whitmore Park, 125 South Cleveland St, play area, picnic area, restrooms

- Mountain View Park, 2052 West Mountain View Rd, play area, picnic area, rest rooms

- PCEI Nature Center, 1040 Rodeo Dr, 208-882-1444, www.pcei.org/nature-center/, dawn to dusk

  Nature trails and wetlands

- Robinson Lake park, 5168 Robinson Park Rd, take 6th St E to Mountain View Dr left for 2m to Robinson Lake Rd, 208-883-5709, 7am-10pm, no fee

- Skate Park, 1515 E D St, skate park, restrooms, play area

- UI Arboretum & Botanical Gardens, 1200 West Palouse River Dr, webpages.uidaho.edu/arboretum/, dawn-dusk, free, 1.3m trail

UI Arboretum

(Wikimedia Commons, creative commons attribution by cheryl.reed)

- Virgil Phillips Farm, 4709 Hwy. 95, 5m out of Moscow, phillipsfarm.org, 7am to sunset, hiking trails, ponds, restrooms, picnic tables

  The large farm and wilderness area is home to many animals including black bear and elk, moose and deer.

*Guides and Tours*

- Idaho Native Plant Society, White Pines chapter, www.whitepineinps.org, regular events highlighting the plant life in Northern Idaho, see schedule on website.

- Palouse Audubon, www.palouseaudubon.org, field trips and lectures are open to the public, website has calendar and description

*Activities*

- Hamilton-Lowe Aquatic Center, 830 N Mountain View, 208-882-7665, picnic tables, wifi

  Water slides, playground, lazy river, lap pool

- Palouse Ice Rink, 1021 Harold St, 208-882-7188, www.palouseicerink.com

*Biking*

- See hiking below for biking trails

- Description of bike routes in the area can be found at http://www.pullmanchamber.com/visit-pullman/things-to-do-in-pullman/pedaling-the-palouse/

- Paradise Creek Bicycles, 513 S Main, 208-882-0703, paradisecreekbikes.com, 9am-7pm, $10 hour, $30 a day

- Mountain Bike in Moscow, check out the website for extensive listings of mountain biking in the Moscow area, bikemoscow.org

*Hiking/Walking*

- Bill Chipman Palouse Trail, Perimeter Dr and the Moscow/Pullman Hwy, 8m paved path connects to Paradise Path and Latah Trail, restrooms on trail, interpretive signs

- Downtown Moscow Walking, download brochure at http://media.wix.com/ugd/c533b2_d5190b86b67e5a962a69a773f1f882fa.pdf

- Idler's Rest, 6th St E for one mile to Mountain View Dr left for 3m to a fork in the road and then turn right onto Idler's Rest Rd .5m, www.pcei.org/idlers_rest.htm

  Several trails through Cedar forest or grassland

- Latah Trail, connects Moscow with Troy, www.latahtrailfoundaiton.org, 22m trail

  Restrooms and picnic tables are available along the trail.

  *Media Connection, brochure about trail*
  *http://www.latahtrailfoundation.org/uploads/LatahTrailBrochure13PROOF11*
  *weba.pdf*

- Paradise Path, 1.5m trail between the University of Idaho campus and downtown, connects to Latah trail

- Residential Moscow Tour, download brochure at http://media.wix.com/ugd/c533b2_d4460a213027b22d460c8029648ff645.pdf

## Kids

- Bonkerz Indoor Play Center, 2305 S Main, 208-596-4320

## Culture and the Arts

- Appaloosa Museum and Heritage Center, 2720 W Pullman Rd, 208-882-5578, 8am-5pm, closed Sun.

  Exhibits about horse breeding with horse viewing in the summer. Exhibits also explain how the Appaloosa were related to the Nez perce.

- Idaho Repertory Theatre, 6th and Stadium Dr, 208-885-6465, www.uidaho.edu/class/irt

- Latah County Historical Museum, 327 E Second St, 208-882-1004, 9am-5pm Tues-Fri.

  Exhibits on Latah history

- The McConnell Mansion Museum, 110 S Adams St, 208-882-1004, 10-4pm Tues-Sat, self-guided tour http://www.latahcountyhistoricalsociety.org/#!mansiontour/c23eu

- Moscow Artwalk, June 17-Sept 10

- UI Prichard Art Gallery, 415 S Main St, 208-885-3586, www.uidaho.edu/caa/galleries/prichardartgallery, 10-8, closed on Mon, with seasonal hours

  Features a variety of changing exhibitions of all types of visual arts of the Northwest.

*Wine, Beer and Cocktails*
- *Bucer's Coffee House Pub, 201 S Main St, 208-882-5216, bucerspub.com, 7am-11pm, closed Sun,

  House roasted coffee, pastries, sandwiches and beer and wine. Live music Thurs-Sat.

- Camas Prairie Winery, 110 S Main St, 208-882-0214, camasprairiewinery.com, 12-6:30pm

  Tasting room includes small tastes of wines, wines by the glass and beer.

- Palouse Touring LLC, 855-829-4487, www.palousetouring.com, winery and brewery tours

- The Perch, 509 University Ave, 208-596-4479, 10am-2am, bar

*Coffee and Tea*
- The Bean Farm, 503 Troy Rd, 425-861-7964

- Botticelli Espresso, 1716 W Pullman Rd, 208-883-5360

- *Bucer's Coffee House Pub, 201 S Main St, 208-882-5216, bucerspub.com, 7am-11pm, closed Sun,

  House roasted coffee, from scratch pastries, homemade desserts, sandwiches and beer and wine. Also serves Ferdinand's local WSU creamery ice cream.

- Cafe Artista, 218 S Main St, 208-882-1324, cafeartistamoscow.com, 7am-7pm, serves Stumptown coffee and republic of tea

  Pastries and beverages with comfortable living room type seating

- Dutch Bros Coffee, 321 N Main St, 208-819-6030

- One World Cafe, 533 S Main St, 208-883-3537, owc-moscow.com, live music, beer and wine, wifi

  Sandwiches, pastries and breakfast options like granola and eggs.

- Red Star Coffee Company, 1046 W Pullman Rd, 208-892-8007, facebook page updated regularly, 5am-9pm, drive thru

- Retro Espresso, 1102 S Main, drive thru espresso stand serving locally roasted coffee and pastries

## Bakery and Treats

- See Bloom (below) and Bucer's Coffee House (above) for bakery items.

- Cowgirl Chocolates, 428 W 3rd St, 208-882-4908, www.cowgirlchocolates.com, 10-5:30pm, closed Sun.

- Panhandle Artisan Bread Co, 630 N Almond St, 208-882-5999, www.panhandlebread.com, 10-6pm Closed Sun and Mon

- Wheatberries Bake Shop, 531 S Main St, 208-882-4618, closed

## Breakfast

- *Bloom Cafe, 403 S Main St, 208-882-4279, moscowbloom.com, 8am-2pm and 5-10 on Sunday, under $15

  Use homemade bread in their dishes. Try the French Toast or a grilled cheese. Salads, soup and egg dishes. Also sells donuts

- Breakfast Club, 501 S Main St, 308-882-6481, facebook page updated regularly, 6am-2pm, under $15

  Some incredibly rich breakfast options like huckleberry French Toast, waffles with whipped cream and chocolate or red velvet waffles. Also, eggs, salad, sandwiches.

## Casual Dining

- Firehouse Grill & Pub, 1710 W Pullman Rd, 208-882-9797, facebook page, under $20

- Big menu with lots of choices from burgers to pasta, from fish to steak from wraps to salads

- *Gnosh, 215 S Main, 208-882-7830, moscowgnosh.com, under $20, wine and beer (big list)

  Small menu with flavorful dishes like hand cut fries with gravy and goat cheese, fish and chips, burgers with bacon comopote or cider steamed clams.

- Loco Grinz Hawaiian BBQ, 113 N Main St, 208-883-4463, closed?

- Insanewich, 115 E 2nd St, 208-882-2008, closed

- La Casa Lopez, 415 S Main St, 208.883-0536, lacasalopez.com, 11am-10pm, full bar, under $20

  Huge menu of Mexican food with both traditional and more unexpected dishes. Almost any dish you imagine on a Mexican menu is on this menu from Chimichangas to Tortas, from Burritos to combination plates, pasta to eggs. Big servings.

- *Maialina Pizzeria Napoletana, 602 South Main St, 208-882-2694, www.maialinapizzeria.com, facebook page updated regularly, occasional live music, 11:30-10pm, beer and wine, under $20

  Small menu of specially prepared Italian dishes including mostly pizza but also a few entrees (chicken, steak, fish) and a variety of antipasta and salad. Upscale pizza. Good Lunch specials.

- Mikey's Greek Gyros, 527 S Main St, 208-882-0780, 11am-8pm, under $5

  Traditional Gyro place with a small selection of apps and salads.

- Mingles Bar and Grill, 102 S Main, 208-882-2050, minglesbarngrill.com, facebook page updated regularly, 11am-2am, under $15

  Televisions, pool tables, dart boards and shuffle board make this as much an entertainment venue as a restaurant. Food includes a bit of everything (lots of it fried) including sandwiches, burgers, salads, wings, fries and a variety of brunch dishes.

- Moscow Alehouse, 226 West 6th St, 208-882-2739, facebook page updated regularly, under $15, operated by Coeur d'Alene brewhouse

- Hearty pub fare like meatball subs, burgers and seasoned fries, onions rings and wings

- Moscow Bagel & Deli, 310 S Main, 208-882-5242, moscowbagel.com, 7am-3am, closes early on Sunday, wifi,

- New York Johnnys Hot dogs and Sandwiches, by the fountain in Friendship square and at the Golf Course at U of I, nyjohnnys.com, 11am-3pm

- Patty's Mexican Kitchen, 450 W 6th St, 208-883-3984, pattysmexicankitchen.com, facebook page updated regularly, 10am-10pm, website didn't work, full bar

  Upscale Mexican

- Pizza Perfection, 428 W Third St, 208-882-1111, pizzaperfection.com, delivery, chain

- Wingers Roadhouse, 1484 S Blaine St, 208-882-9850, www.wingers.info/l_moscow.html, 7am-9pm, beer and wine, chain

*Upscale Dining*
- *Nectar Restaurant and Wine Bar, 105 W 6th St, 208-882-5914, moscownectar.com, 4-10pm, most dishes are under $20, wine and beer

  Small menu with finely prepared comfort food like mac and cheese made with Cougar Gold, pan roasted chicken and meatloaf.

- Sangria Grille, 2124 W Pullman Rd, 208-882-2693, www.sangriagrille.com, 4:30-10pm, most dishes under $20

  South American emphasis with salads, appetizers, pasta, fish and meat in traditional preparations that use local ingredients. The menu is quite eclectic and probably the most unusual in town.

*Camping*
- Robinson Lake park, 5168 Robinson Park Rd, take 6th St E to Mountain View Dr left for 2m to Robinson Lake Rd, 208-883-5709, RV and Tent camping, hook up, picnic tables, vault toilets, no showers

*Lodging*
- Anderson on Eighth, 705 E Eight St, 208-882-8386, can't find anything

- Andriette's Bed, Book and Bicycle, 115 N Polk St, 208-882-2756, andriettes.blogspot.com, $380

  Guests share living room, kitchen and baths, with separate sleeping areas.

- Bella Vista Farm, 1045 Schultz Rd, 208-301-3588, thebellavistafarm.com, $125 for room with private bath, $375 for farmhouse, wifi

- Browne Block Guesthouse Above the Winery, 112 S Main, 208-883-3661, browneblockgruesthouse.com, sleeps 4, wifi, kitchen, laundry, $110

  Located in the heart of downtown, this solar powered apartment is comfortable and casual

- Campus View Cottage, 906 West C St., 208-310-0261, $160, sleeps 6

- Granite Grove Bed & Breakfast, 3045 Hwy. 95 S, 208-882-8391, www.granitegrove.com/home.html, $85 includes full country breakfast, fishing, wifi

  Vintage rooms with iron bedsteads and bright quilts

- Haystack B & B, 208-301-4463, haystackbandb.blogspot.com, $97, continental breakfast included, wifi, dog friendly, book at airbnb.com

- Idaho Inn, 645 W Pullman Rd, 208-885-1480, www.idahoinn.com, wifi, complimentary continental breakfast, air con, $60

  Clean bright typical motel rooms

- Little Green Guesthouse, 1020 S Adams, 208-669-1654, littlegreenguesthouse.com, wifi, kitchen

- Little River Bed and Breakfast, 1101 Lyon Rd, 5m from downtown Moscow, 208-882-1975, www.littleriverbedanadbreakfast.net, Yurt and motel room with one bathroom 20ft away (bathroom is private, not shared), $90-120

  Lovely outside areas border a small creek,

- MaryJanesFarm Bed & Breakfast, 888-750-6004, www.maryjanesfarm.org/bb/, not currently accepting reservations

- Meadowinds Bed & Breakfast, 2493 Blaine Rd, 208-882-7907, www.meadowinds.org, $100-200

- Palouse Inn, 101 Baker St, 360-4802049, www.palouseinn.com,

  Low end basic motel

- Paradise View Bed & Breakfast, 1005 Joyce Rd, 360-480-2049, www.paradiseviewbb.com, wifi, laundry, 2 rooms with private baths, one room sleeps 4, dog friendly, $85-175

  Rooms are simple with wood floors and bed frames with white spreads. Common area includes a big screen TV and an outdoor patio is also available. Lovely views from the rooms just outside the town.

- Peterson Barn Guesthouse, 847 Travois Way, 208-882-4620, www.petersonbarn.com, wifi, $110-130, sleeps 4

Guesthouse, made by hand, is on a farm off the latah Trail. 750ft of living space including a loft, kitchen and living room all in lovely woods and antique furnishings (including an antique stove). No air conditioning.

- Rose Ridge Farm Bed and Breakfast, 1137 Paradise Ridge Rd, gone?

- Sixth Street Retreat, 441 E 6th St, 208-669-0763, sixthstreetretreat.com, 3 furnished apartments, wifi, laundry, air con, sleeps 4, $95-125

- Wylie Lauder House Bed & Breakfast, 1320 Deakin Ave, 208-883-5593, wylielauderhouse.blogspot.com, $135 with full breakfast,

## Viola GPS: 46.50N, 117.01 W ; Elevation: 2631 ft

### Getting Oriented
- Not much here

- East of Hwy. 95, just E of the Washington border and N of Moscow

## Potlatch GPS: 46.55N, 116.53 W ; Elevation: 2546 ft

*Learn More About It, visitors here would never guess that this was once the site of the country's biggest lumber mills. Today, Potlatch is a commuter town for Moscow. In 1981, the lumber mills shut down and the town emptied out. But it has a long history, dating from its beginning in 1905. It's the quintessential "Company Town"*

### Getting Oriented
- East of Hwy. 95 and N of Moscow on Hwy. 6.

### Practicalities
- Visitor Information

  www.cityofpotlatch.org

  Palouse Ranger Station, 1700 Hwy. 6, 208-875-1131, 7:30-4pm Mon-Fri.

  Mineral Mountain Rest Area, on Hwy. 95 between MP 370-371, restrooms, picnic tables

- Grocery

  Floyd's Harvest Foods, 150 6th St, 208-875-0616, 8am-8pm, full service grocery with hot deli

  Four Star Supply, 120 6th St, 208-875-1251, gas, grocery, deli

- Laundry

  Dale's Wagon Wheel and Laundromat, 220 6th St, 208-875-0199, 10-2am

- Library

  Potlatch Public Library, 1010 Onaway Rd, 208-875-1036, latahlibrary.org

*Activities*
- Potlatch Historical Society, 195 6th St, located in City Hall

  Small history collection

- Walking Tour of Potlatch Commercial District, download brochure at
  http://media.wix.com/ugd/c533b2_0e12b344fd29d40bbf1aedb658488286.pdf

- Walking Tour of Potlatch Neighborhoods, download brochure at
  http://media.wix.com/ugd/c533b2_091a0837d1d8867cc4ca298d35a9c536.pdf

- White Pine Scenic Byway (Hwy. 3 to Hwy. 6), day use only, see listing under
  St Maries

*Coffee*
- PS Espresso & More, 150 Hwy. 6, 208-875-0235, 5am-5pm, closed Sun,
  espresso, milkshakes

*Dining*
- Dad's Diner, 5497 Hwy. 95, 208-875-1362

  Hole in the wall diner with traditional American meals

- Dale's Wagon Wheel, 220 6th St, 208-875-0199, facebook page, 10-2am

- Silver Saddle Saloon and Grille, 509 Pine St, 208-875-0506, 11am-12am,
  facebook page

  Burgers

*Lodging*
- Laird House Bed and Breakfast, 310 Cedar St, 208-875-0688, reserve on
  Airbnb.com, $85, accommodations for up to 6, 1 bathroom

*Camping*
- North Shore Campground, 5m W of Trout Creek on old Hwy. 200, 13 sites,
  picnic area, drinking water, vault toilets, boat ramp, fishing

- Campground, 11m East of Idaho border on Hwy. 200, MM 11.2, picnic tables, fire rings, potable water, flush toilets, $10, reserve at www.recreation.gov, fishing

- Scenic 6 Park, 125 6th St, 208-875-1117, 22 sites, play park area, picnic area, showers, restrooms

This area used to be the home of the Potlatch Corp lumber mill for 80 years.

**Onaway** GPS: 46.55N, 116.53W ; Elevation: 2621 ft, nothing here

**Princeton** GPS: 46.54N, 116.50W ; Elevation: 2516 ft

*Getting Oriented*
- On Hwy. 6

*Dining*
- Gold Hill Cafe, 3470 Hwy. 6, 208-875-0138

**Harvard** GPS: 46.55N, 116.43W ; Elevation 2575 ft

*Getting Oriented*
- On Hwy. 6, nothing here

**Bovill** GPS 46.51N, 116.23 W; Elevation: 2874 ft

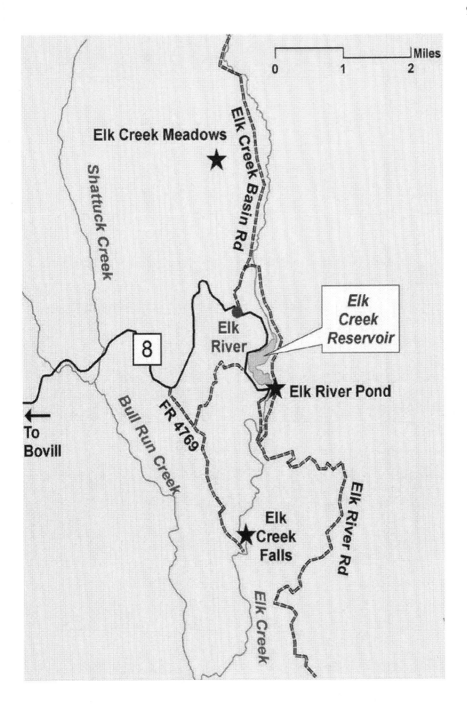

**Map of Elk River**
(Map is From Idaho Fish and Game)

*Getting Oriented*
- On Hwy. 3

- This small town was once a thriving community, central to tourism in the area for those seeking hunting, fishing and the Bovill Hotel. The Bovills were Lord and Lady Bovill who lived here until 1911. Logging brought in a rougher sort of people and the Bovills left.

*Practicalities*
- Bovill Community Library, 310 1st Ave, 208-826-3451, latahlibrary.org

*Parks*
- Moose Creek Park, 3m W off of Hwy. 3/8 on FR 281

*Activities*
- Bovill City RV Park, 201 3rd Ave, full hookups, pull thru sites, fishing, pets ok

- Elk Creek Falls Recreation Area, Hwy. 8 and follow signs to Elk River, turning at Elk Creek Falls Rd, to FR 1452, restrooms, picnic tables, hiking trail

  Series of waterfalls plunging 300 ft into a forest canyon, the tallest fall in Idaho. The falls tumble through three canyons of basalt. 1m trail is a historic wagon road. 3.5m trail takes visitors through a rough trail to the highest fall.

- Idaho Whitetail Guides, 208-826-3651, www.idahowhitetailguides.com, big game hunting guides

- Perkins Cedar Grove, FR 382, 3/4m shady trail

  Old growth cedar includes a 500year old tree

*Dining*
- Bailey's Bar, 104 Main St, 208-826-3504

*Camping*
- Moose Creek Reservoir, W of Bovill on Hwy. 8, 24 sites, fire ring and picnic table, potable water, vault toilets, swimming, fishing

# Deary GPS 46.48N, 116.33 W; 2874 ft

*Getting Oriented*
- At the intersection of Hwy. 8 and Hwy. 3

- Once a thriving logging community, Deary was originally settled by Scandinavians and was named for William Deary, the manager of the Potlatch Lumber Company.

*Practicalities*
- Grocery

  Crossroads Convenience Store and Gas Station, 700 2nd Ave, 208-877-1606

  White Pine Foods, 402 2nd Ave, 208-877-1310

- Library

  Deary Community Library, 304 2nd Ave, 208-877-1664, latahlibrary.org

*Dining*
- Helmer Store and Cafe, 2130 Hwy. 8, 208-877-1468, 9am-7pm, food and groceries

  Burgers, Fish

- Ireland's Kozy Korner, 401 2nd Ave, 208-877-7750, facebook page, 8am-8pm

  Mexican food on Tuesday,

**Troy** GPS 46.44N, 116.46 W; Elevation 2487ft

*Getting Oriented*
- Hwy. 8

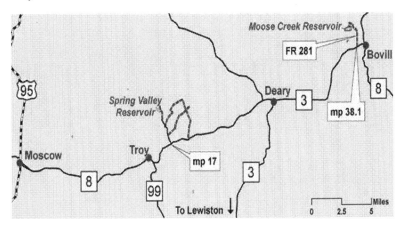

# Map of Moscow to Bovill
(From fishandgame.idaho.gov)

*Practicalities*
- Visitor Information

Troyidaho.net

Plains/Thompson Falls Ranger District Station, Hwy. 200 to Clayton Street East, 406-826-3821

- Grocery

  Sunset Mart, 3990 Hwy. 8, 208-835-6761, sunsetmarts.com, 5am-11pm

  Troy Market, 339 S Main St, 208-835-3111

- Restrooms

  Troy Community Library, 402 S Main St, 208-835-4311

*Activities*
- City Park, on Hwy. 8 on the W side of town, Latah Trail runs by the park, restrooms

- Latah Trail, accessed at the City Park (see Latah Trail under Latah County)

- Callahan Historic Trail (#153), take Callahan Creek Rd 427 for 1 mile, 2m trail

  Follows an old railroad grade and has interpretive signs and benches.

- Spring Valley Reservoir, Hwy. 8 to Spring Valley Rd, picnic tables, boat docks, restrooms, fishing, swimming, nature trail

*Dining*
- *The Mugshots Filling Station, 504 S Main, 208-835-2300, fillingstationidaho.weebly.com, facebook page, 5am-4pm, closed Sun-Mon, drive thru and walk in

  Small town cafe with coffee, homemade pastries and sandwiches in a refurbished gas station.

## Kendrick/Juliaetta GPS: 46.36N, 116.39W ; Elevation: 1240ft

*Getting Oriented*
- At the intersection of hwy. 99 and Hwy. 3

*Practicalities*
- Visitor Information

  www.kendrick-juliaetta.org

- Library

Juliaetta Community Library, wifi 24/7

- Grocery

  Juliaetta market, 1051 Main St, Juliaetta, 208-276-3281, deli and groceries, laundry

  Phil's Family Foods, 507 E Main St, Kendrick 289-5957,

*Activities*
- Bethany Memorial Chapel, 6m NE of Kendrick

  Small chapel built in 1905 by Norwegian homesteaders with hand carved pews, alter rail and pulpit

Wikipedia, GNU free documentation license, courtesy of Robbiegiles

- Castle Museum, 191 State St, 208-276-7174, open by appointment

  The castle was built in 1906 to resemble those in Scotland. Its collections are focused on pioneer living at the turn of the century.

- Centennial Park, Juliaetta, restrooms with art mosaic mural, access to Ed Corkhill trail (see below), small butterfly garden

- Ed Corkhill Trail, parallel to Hwy. 3 between Kendrick and Juliaetta, 5.3m asphalt trail along the Potlatch River, might see Osprey or Bald Eagles along the trail

- Kendrick's Memorial park, restrooms, access to Ed Corkhill Trail (see above)

*Wine and Beer*
- Colter's Creek Winery, 308 Main St, 208-276-3342, www.coltercreek.com 4-9pm, tasting 4-6 Thurs-Sun., beer, wine and light bites

*Dining*
- First Bank of Pizza, 3rd and Main, Juliaetta, 208-276-7061

## Clearwater County

*Getting Oriented*
- Located in the middle of the Panhandle. There are very few towns. Dworshank Reservoir is on the SW side.

### Elk River GPS: 46.46N, 116. 10 W ; Elevation: 2854 ft

*Getting Oriented*
- Hwy 8 runs through town

*Practicalities*
- Visitor Information

  www.elkriveridaho.com

- Library

  Elk River Free Library, 203 Main St, 208-826-3539

- Grocery

  Elk River Lodge and General Store, 208-826-3299, www.elkriverlodge.net,

*Activities*
- Elk Butte Adventures, 208-826-3632, www.elkbutteadventures.com

  snowmobile rentals and ATV rental

- Elk River Backcountry Byway, begins at Orofino at Hwy. 7 and ends in Bovill, 57 mile route, mostly paved

  Pass ranches and forests as you wind into the backcountry including a crossing on a suspension bridge over the Dworkshak reservoir.

- Elk Creek Reservoir, 3m before Hwy. 8 at Elk River, turn Right on FR 4769, vault toilets, picnic table,

- CT Camp, 4 sites, vault toilet, picnic tables

- Dent Bridge, S on Dent Rd, 1550 ft long bridge, 500 ft high

- Giant Cedar Grove Trailhead and The Giant Cedar Tree, from Elk River take FR 382 for 10m and turn right on FS 4764 (Upper Basin Rd), part of the road is gravel, vault toilet, .5m, largest tree in North America east of the Cascade-Sierra Crest

- Jarvey Park, one mile East of Elk River, 5 sites, restrooms, picnic tables

- Merrill Park, one mile East of Elk River, 15 sites, vault toilets, picnic tables

- Morris/Perkins Cedar Grove, North Basin Rd out of Elk River and follow signs, keeping right at intersections, .5m trail

## Dining

- Log Inn, 112 S Front St, 208-826-3300, www.loginnelkriver.com, 12pm-close, closed on Tues. under $20

  Ribs and Steaks, burgers and fried stuff. Burgers are hand formed on site. Pizza is also made on site. Ice cream

## Camping

- Dent Acres Recreation Site, Dent Rd S, water, hook ups, fishing, picnic area, flush toilets and showers, dumping, fee

- Elk River Campground, Hwy. 8 and then North onto FR 382 and East on FR 1705, at 6000ft elevation, drinking water, hookups, vault toilets, fishing, hiking

- Moose Cove, backside of Elk Creek Reservoir, 10 sites, porta potty, picnic tables

- Partridge Creek Campground, NE of the Reservoir, 10 sites

## Lodging

- Elk River Lodge, 210 S Main St, 208-826-3299, www.elkriverlodge.net, boarding house style lodging with men and women's bathrooms, wifi, $59-99

Common area with kitchen to share and seven bedrooms

## Peck GPS: 46.28N, 116.25 W; Elevation: 1089 feet

### Getting Oriented
- Just N of Orofino on the N side of Clearwater River

### Practicalities
- Library

  Prairie River Library District, 217 N Main St, 208-486-6161, prairieriver.lili.org, 10-6

### Activities
- Boulder Creek Outfitters, 2158 Little Canyon Rd, 208-486-6903, bouldercreekoutfitters.com, big game hunting, long range shooting school
- Little Canyon Shooting Preserve, Pheasant and Chukar hunts, sporting clay course, continental shoots, lodging and dining on site

### Dining
- Canyon Inn Bar & Grill, 20289 Big Canyon Rd., 208-486-6070, canyoninnrvpark.com, www.canyoninnbarandgrill.com, 5-9 Mon-Tues, 8am-9p Wed-Fri, 7am-9pm Sat-Sun, full bar

  Burgers, pancakes and large servings of American food

### Camping
- Canyon Inn and RV Park, 20289 Big Canyon Rd, 208-486-6070, full hook ups, water

## Ahsahka GPS: 46.30N, 116.19 W; Elevation: 994 feet

### Getting Oriented
- Just N of Orofino on the N side of Clearwater River off Hwy 7

### Practicalities

### Activities
- Dworshak National Fish Hatchery Complex, 4147 Ahsahka Rd, Hwy. 7 at Ahsahka Rd, 208-476-4591, 9am-3pm

  The large fishery raises cold-water fish species including Salmon and Trout. Self guided tours are available and brochures at the site help interpret the process.

*Media Connection, Fish and Wildlife Service has a brochure on the hatchery, http://www.fws.gov/dworshak/pdf/Dworshak%20Complex.pdf*

- Dworkshak State Park, 9934 Freeman Creek, 208-476-5994, 105 sites, 4 cabins, showers, dump station, flush toilets, boating, fishing, trails, archery course

  850 acre park with meadows, woods and water. There are 12 miles of hiking trails

- The Big Eddy Trail, starts from the upper launch area parking lot at Freeman Creek, 20m RT

- US Fish and Wildlife Services, Hwy. 7, 208-476-4591

- High Country Inn Guides, 70 High Country Lane, 208-476-7570, www.thehighcountryinn.com, fishing

*Dining*
- Woodlot Tavern and Cafe, 56 Northfork Dr, 208-476-4320, 7am-8pm, closed

  Home cooked meal including burgers, soup, roast beef and fresh cut fries. Shakes and malts as well.

*Campground*
- Dent Acres Campground, 208-476-1255, 43 sites, dump station, showers, flush toilets, picnic tables, boat laundh, playground

*Lodging*
- High Country Inn, 70 High Country Lane, 208-476-7570, www.thehighcountryinn.com, dining, wifi, hot tub, 2 cabins and 2 rooms, kitchen access, laundry, hiking trail, $89-275 including full breakfast

**Orofino** GPS: 46.29N, 116.15 W; Elevation: 1030 feet

*Getting Oriented*

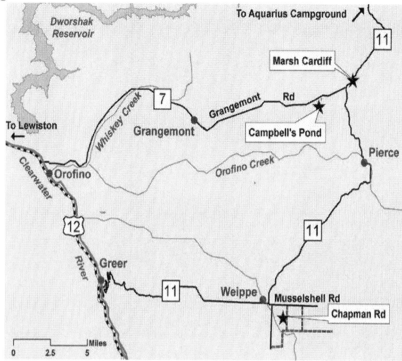

## Map of Orofino, Greer, Grangemont, Pierce Area

From fishandgame.idaho.gov

- Off Hwy. 12 to the E side of Clearwater River. Orofino stretches along the banks of the river S of the Dworshak Reservoir.

- Orofino is the home of the Idaho Correctional Institution which takes up a big swath of land to the N of the town.

*Practicalities*

- Grocery

  Barney's Harvest Foods, 13030 Hwy. 12, 208-476-3413

  Frontier Foods, 218 College Ave, 208-476-5215, full service grocery store

  Glenwood IGA, 1130 Michigan Ave, 208-476-3011

  Orofino Real Food Country Store, 206 Johnson Ave, 208-476-3600

Sunset Mart, Michigan Ave, 208-476-7145, convenient mart

- Visitor Information

- North Fork Ranger Station, 12730 B Hwy. 12, 208-476-4541, 8-4:30pm Mon-Fri

- Website: www.orofino.com

- Library

Clearwater Public Library, 402 Michigan Ave, 208-476-3411

*Activities*

- Bald Mountain Ski Area, 1070 Bald Mountain Rd, 208-464-2311, skibaldmountain.com, located in Pierce, a free bus runs visitors from The Glenwood IGA to the ski area.

- Clearwater Historical Museum, 315 College Ave, 208-476-5033, clearwaterhumeum.org, 12:30-5:30

History of Clearwater County including information on the Nez Perce and the Lewis and Clark expedition

- Canoe Camp Historic Site, .5m W on Hwy. 12

Park's location on the lake makes for great views and water activities. Here, Lewis and Clark worked with the Nez Perce to carve canoes to take them to the Pacific Ocean. The park includes an interpretive panel and attractive grounds.

- The Guide Shop & Clearwater Drifters, 175 140th St, 208-476-3531, www.theguideshop.com, fishing guides, shuttle service

- Harper's Bend Recreation Site, 10 m W of Orofino at MM 33, boat ramp, vault toilet

- Jarrett's Guide Service, 208-476-3791, www.wefishhere.com, fishing guides

- Lewis and Clark National Historic Trail, roughly along Hwy. 12, between Orofino and Lolo Pass

Lewis and Clark used this trail to cross the Bitterroot Mountains

*Media Connection, download a brochure detailing this trail at http://www.fs.usda.gov/Internet/FSE_DOCUMENTS/stelprdb5410770.pdf*

*Coffee*

- Koala Kaffe, 10280 Hwy. 12, 208-827-2656, facebook page updated regularly, 5:30-5pm,

*Dining*

- Augie's Deli, 202 Johnson Ave, 208-476-5450, facebook page updated regularly, 9am-5pm

  Soup and sandwiches

- China Palace, 214 Johnson Ave, 208-476-7721

- Crystal Cafe, 128 Johnson Ave, gone?

- Dining of the Edge, 625 Main St, 208-476-7805, diningontheedge.com, 11am-9pm, inside and outside dining with views of the river, under $20

  Prime rib, steaks, chicken and fish. Large lunch men and small dinner menu

- Fiesta En Jalisco, 203 Johnson Ave, 208-476-7506, fiestenjalisco.net, under $20, chain

- Pizza Factory, 307 Michigan Ave, 208-476-5519, orofino.pizzafactory.com, chain

- Ponderosa Restaurant and Brass Rail Lounge, 220 Michigan Ave, 208-476-4818, www.ponderosacafe.com, 5am-10pm, under $20

  Full service old timey restaurant with big booths and comfortable furnishings. Serving traditional American food including homemade pies, ice cream, and broasted chicken.

- Ronatta's Cakery, 221 Main, 208-476-4400, ronattascakery.com, website gone

- Riverside Lanes Coffee Shop, 10820 hwy. 12, gone?

  Bowling Alley with burgers and fries

*Camping*

- Canoe Camp RV Park, 14224 Hwy. 12, 208-476-7530, www.canoecamprvpark.com, 28 sites, full hook ups, potable water, restrooms, espresso shop, gift shop

- Clearwater Crossing RV Park, 500 Riverfront Ave, 208-476-4760, www.clearwatercrossingrvpark.com, 49 sites, wifi, showers, restrooms, laundry, picnic tables

- Pink House Recreation Site, 5m W of Orofino on Hwy. 12, 15 sites, full hookup, picnic tables, drinking water, vault and flush toilets, fee

Camping area is right on the river though must sites are situated off the river.

## Lodging
- Many Chain options

- Helgeson Place Suites, 125 Johnson Ave, 208-476-5729, helgesonhotel.com, 20 suites, kitchen, wifi, complimentary breakfast, $59-99

Historic hotel with contemporary style rooms

- Konkolville Motel, 2600 Michigan Ave, 3m from downtown, 208-476-5584, www.konkolvillemotel.com, $55-85, continental breakfast, wifi, outdoor pool, hot tub, laundry, pets welcome

Typical motel rooms with drive up parking. They offer grill your own steak dinners.

- Riverside Motel, 10506 Hwy. 12, 208-476-5711, www.theriversidemotel.com, $55-65

    Basic motel some with kitchenettes

- Wild Rooster Ranch, 4262 Dent Bridge Rd, 208-476-3317, www.wildroostervacationranch.com, ranch house rental

- White Pine Motel, 222 Brown Ave, 208-476-7093, www.whitepinemotel.com, wifi, air con

Basic motel

## Lochsa/Powell GPS 46.34N, 114.43W Elevation: 5874 ft

## Getting Oriented
- on Hwy. 12 at the Montana border

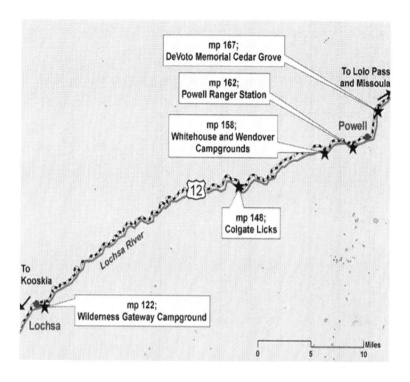

## Map of Lochsa to Powell

From fishandgame.idaho.gov (see additional map of Hwy. 12 under Lochsa/Powell)

*Practicalities*

- Visitor Information

  Powell Ranger Station, in Lolo MT, 208-942-1132

  Lochsa Historical Ranger Station, MM 121.6 Hwy. 12, Memorial Day-Labor Day, fishing

  Staffed by retired rangers, this remote forest ranger station was built in the 1920's. Interpretive exhibits and walking tour available.

*Activities*

- Colgate Licks, MM 148 on Hwy. 12, .5m recreation trail

  This open glade has mineral deposits and a recreation trail through pine, fir, and cedar with interpretive stations explaining the affects of fire.

- Devoto Grove, MM 165 Hwy. 12,

  Old growth cedar grove with interpretive boardwalks

- Jerry Johnson Hot Springs, park at Warm Springs pack bridge at MM 152 on the N side of Hwy. 12, cross the highway and the Lochsa River and stay on the west main trail for 1m to the first pool, another .5m to the second pool

These pools are often crowded and often with nude bathers. A nearby cold creek allows for cooling off. Pools reach 104 degrees.

- Lolo Motorway, on Hwy. 12, turn E on Glenwood Rd (FR 100) to Lolo Creek Rd to FR 500 to Lolo Motor Way (FR 569), July-Sept. This is a winding kind of difficult ride that will take a couple of hours and is partially unsurfaced. Once you get to the Lolo Motorway, it is a one way road not suitable for low-clearance vehicles.

*Learn More About It: Imagine, as you drive this convoluted route, that the Nez Perce once traversed a similar route as they fled Captain Whipple's troops in July 1877. The Soldiers finally catch up with the Nez Perce for what has been called the Clearwater Battle. After the battle, the Nez Perce flee and encounter the Soldiers at various points through July. At the end of July, the Nez Perce move into Montana where the soldiers continue to harass them where ultimately they meet in mid-August at the Big Hole Battlefield.*

*Media Connection: for information on Lewis and Clark's crossing through this area, download the brochure at http://www.idahostateatv.org/publications/Lewis__Clark_on_the_Lolo_Trail.p df*

- Lolo Pass Visitor Center, 21200 Hwy. 12 W (MM 174), 208-942-3113, 7:30-4pm Thurs-Mon, .25m interpretive trail, restrooms open 24 hours, picnic tables

Historical, natural and general information in the area

## Dining
- *Lochsa Lodge, 115 Powell Rd, 208-942-3405, www.lochsalodge.com, indoor and outdoor dining, open all year every day

Homemade soups and desserts and full menu

## Camping
- Powell Campground, MM 162 Hwy. 12, 3800ft elevation, water, flush and vault toilets, hookups, picnic area, fishing

Access the Powell Complex trail, 1.5m trail. The campground is located on the Lochsa River and is heavily forested.

## Lodging
- Lochsa Lodge, 115 Powell Rd, 208-942-3405, www.lochsalodge.com, pet friendly, rustic and modern cabins and lodge rooms, $68-115

Quilted beds in comfortable, attractive western style rooms.

## Greer GPS 46.23N, 116.10 W, Elevation: 1102 ft

*Learn More About It: Greer was once the spot of Dunwell's Ferry. In 1877, the Nez Perce held off the soldiers after the Clearwater Battle as they pursued the Native People.*

### Getting Oriented
- Off Hwy 12, to the East , on the Clearwater river

### Activities
- Bald Mountain Ski Area, 1070 Bald Mountain Rd, 208-464-2311, skibaldmountain.com, located in Pierce, a free bus runs visitors from MaryAnns to the ski area.

- Five Mile Wayside, MM 54.5 on Hwy. 12, interpretive sign

- Gold Rush Historic Byway, Hwy. 11 East, 42.5m

  Rolling fields and grain and then forest along this very winding route once traveled by prospectors in 1860. First part of the road is mostly paved to Weipee with excellent views of the Clearwater Valley into Pierce. The road climbs through switchbacks and then levels out as it passes through the meadows.

- Fraser Park, on the Gold Rush Historic Byway, community park

## Weippe GPS 46.22N, 115.56 W, Elevation: 3015 ft

### Getting Oriented
- Weippe is to the East of hwy., 12 on Hwy. 11

### Practicalities
- Visitor Information

  www.pierce-weippechamber.com/visitor.html

  www.weippe.com

- Grocery

  MaryAnn's Groceries, 316 Main St, 208-435-4213, full service mini grocery

- Laundry

  Timberline Cafe & RV Park, 1022 N Main, 866-284-6237, 7am-9pm

- Library

  Weippe Public Library, 204 Wood St, 208-432-4058, weippelibrary.org

*Activities*

- Gold Rush Historic Byway, 208-435-4406, see above in Greer

- Hilltop Heritage Museum, 617 N Main St, 208-435-4200

- Our Lady of the Woodland Catholic Church, 112 Holmes Dr, this log cabin church was built in 1900, the church is still in use

- Weippe Discovery Center, 204 Wood St, 208-435-4058, weippediscoverycenter.com, nature trails

  Historical murals and a living history display are housed in this building along with the library and a technology center

- Weippe Prairie, MP 17 on Hwy. 11, Camas flowers fill this prairie in the Spring. The Nez Perce met a starving Lewis and Clark here

Camas Flower, from wikipedia Creative Commons Attribution 2.5 Generic
to {{Information |Description={{en|{{en|Common camas or Indian Camas, "Camassia quamash".}}
|Source=*File:Camassia_quamash_(Pursh)_Greene.jpg|Date={{Date|2004|11|20}}
|Author=*File:Camassia_quamash_(Pursh)_Greene.jpg: William & Wilma Follette

*Dining*
- Sherry's Cakes and Flowers, 119 S Main, 208-435-4793, sherryscakes.wix.com

- Timberline Cafe & RV Park, 1022 N Main, 866-284-6237, 7am-9pm

  Salad bar, homemade pies, soup, sandwiches, salad

## Camping

- Watts RV Park, 705 W Pierce St, 208-435-4140, www.pierce-weippechamber.com

## Lodging

- Timberline Cafe & RV Park, 1022 N Main, 866-284-6237

# Pierce GPS 46.29N, 115.47 W, Elevation: 3094ft

## Getting Oriented

- Pierce is on Hwy. 11

  *Did you know? Pierce was one of the first established towns in Idaho in 1860 as men rushed from far and wide to strike it rich. From 1865-1870 this area was largely populated by Chinese immigrants who were miners and businessmen.*

## Practicalities

- Grocery

  S&S Foods, 501 S Main St, 208-464-2332, ssfamilyfoods.com, full service grocery with deli and bakery

- Laundry

  Pierce Laundry, 219 S Main, 208-464-2171

- Library

  *Pierce Free Public Library, 208 S Main St, 208-464-2823, exhibit on the Chinese community who originally settled the area is worth a visit.

## Activities

- Bradbury Logging Museum, 103 S Main St, 208-464-2677, www.pierce-weippechamber.com, 12-4pm

  Historical logging and mining artifacts located in a 1928 cabin.

- Campbell's Pond, Grangemont Rd 1.5m W of the Junction with Hwy. 11, look for the Sportsman Access sign, vault toilets, picnic tables, fishing

- Chinese Hanging Site, MP 27.5 Hwy. 11, here five Chinese men were hung after being accused of killing a merchant.

- Deer Creek Reservoir, 11m N of Pierce on Hwy. 11 and follow signs, fishing 80 acre reservoir is stocked with rainbow and cut-throat trout

- Bald Mountain Ski Area, 1070 Bald Mountain Rd, 4000ft elevation, 208-464-2311, skibaldmountain.com, 9:30-3:30, adult full day is $20, cafe, equipment available for rent, ski and snowboard lessons

  The ski area tops out at 4800 ft and includes 140 acres of terrain with a mix of beginner, intermediate and advanced.

- Pierce Historic Courthouse, 404 S Main St, 208-464-2222

  It's hard to recognize this clapboard building as the courthouse but back in 1860 the local forests provided the material needed to build Idaho's first courthouse.

- Pierce Public Park, on Carle St,

- Pierce-Weippe Area Snowmobile Trails, 300 miles of trails in the Clearwater National Forest

## Dining

- The Vug, 114 S Main St, 208-464-1314

- Pioneer Inn, 412 S Main St, 208-464-1444, www.pioneerinnidaho.com, 8am-9pm, under $15

  Family style restaurant with burgers, salads, sandwiches and steak and chicken meals.

- Timber Inn, 2 S Main St, 208-464-2736, idahotimberinn.com, under $10

  Known for their burgers, they also serve breakfast and lots of fried stuff.

## Lodging

- Cedar Inn, 412 S Main St, 800-450-0250, www.minershanty.net, closed

- The Outback, 211 S Main St, 800-538-1754, www.outbackidaho.com, wifi, free continental breakfast, hot tub, fishing, playground, suites and cabins, $55-125

- Pioneer Inn, 412 S Main St, 208-464-1444, www.pioneerinnidaho.com, wifi

  Rooms in the 1900 inn have been remodeled with simple furnishings and muted colors.

- Timber Inn, 2 S Main St, 208-464-2736, idahotimberinn.com, 5 rooms, wifi, laundry, deck area

Rooms are rustic and simple

## Lewis County

*Getting Oriented*
- The little county of Lewis is centered around Craigmont on Hwy. 95.

## Nezperce GPS: 46.14N, 116.14W ; Elevation: 3215 ft

*Getting Oriented (heading 4)*
- Off Hwy. 64

*Practicalities*
- Visitor Information

  www.cityofnezperce.com

- Grocery

  Midway Foods, 506 OakSt, 208-937-2257

- Library

  Nezperce Library, 602 4th Ave, 208-937-2458

*Activities*
- Nezperce Museum & Historical Society, 9-11:30 and noon-4pm seasonal,

  History and memorabilia of Lewis County including several outdoor exhibits

*Dining*
- Nezperce Cafe, 312 OakSt, 208-937-2265

- Shari's Pizza Plus Pub, 419 Oak St, 208-937-1090

- Serenity Cafe, 312 Oak St, 208-937-2265, serentiyholdings.net

  Cute little local cafe.

*Camping*
- Nezperce RV Park, 502 5th Ave, 208-937-1021

*Lodging*
- Nezperce Hotel, 603 Fourth Ave, 208-937-2265, nezpercehotel.com, 8 rooms, wifi, restaurant on site

**Winchester** GPS: 46.12N, 116.37 W ; Elevation: 3980 ft

*Getting Oriented*
- Off Hwy. 95 on the N edge of Winchester Lake. Business 95 runs through town.

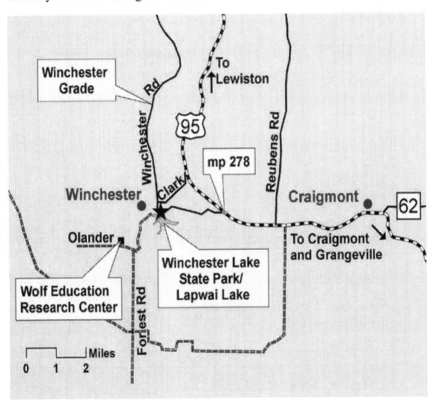

## Map of Winchester and Craigmont
from fishandgame.idaho.gov

*Practicalities*
- Library

  Winchester Library, 314 Nezperce, 208-924-5164, 9am-12-1pm-6pm, Tues, Weds, Thurs, wifi

- Laundry

  The Gateway, 305 Jospeh Ave, 208-924-6831, laundromat,

- Grocery

The Gateway, 305 Joseph Ave, 208-924-6831, laundromat, fish and game licensing

Marshall Meats Center, 402 Nezperce, 208-924-7841, 8am-6pm, closed Sun, also sells alcohol

### Activities

- Winchester Lake State Park, 1786 Forest Rd, 208-924-7563, restrooms, showers, picnic tables, playground, dump station, fishing

- Winchester Museum, 421 Ellis St, 10am Mon, 12-3 Fri--Sat seasonal, or by appointment

   History exhibits, native plant garden

- *Wolf Education & Research Center, 518 Joseph Ave, 888-422-1110, www.wolfcenter.org, facebook page updated regularly, fee

   The first full week in June, the center offers a conference about wolves. Tours are available or self-guided walking. Make reservations on the website.

### Dining

- Calamity's Lake City Cafe, 208-924-6858, 6am-2pm, closed Weds

- Miss Lilys, 304 Joseph Ave, 208-924-0019

- Syls Saloon & Cafe, 317 Nezperce Ave, 208-924-7255, 12-2am

### Lodging

- Minnie Motel, 520 Algoma, 208-924-7784, still here?

- Winchester Lake State Park, 1786 Forest Rd, 208-924-7563, restrooms, showers, dump station, picnic tables, fishing, yurts, 46 campsites

- Winchester Lake Lodge, 214 Joseph Ave, 208-924-6430, www.winchesterlakelodge.com, hot tub, wifi, cabins and lodge rooms, $69-119, no credit cards, property is for sale

   Rooms are decorated with Western themes and feature basic furnishings.

# Reubens GPS: 46.19N, 116.32 W; Elevation: 3527 ft, nothing here

# Slickpoo GPS: 46.19N, 116.42 W; Elevation: 1749 ft, nothing here

# Craigmont GPS: 46.12N, 116.28W ; Elevation: 3740

*Getting Oriented*

- Hwy. 95 runs to the S side of Craigmont. Business 95 goes through downtown and connects with Hwy. 62

*Practicalities*

- Visitor Information

  www.craigmonareachamber.com

- Grocery

  Berrys, 121 West Main, 208-924-5501, 7am-5pm, full service grocery including deli

- Library

- Craigmont Library, 112 West Main, 208-924-5510, 10:3-3:30 Mon, Weds, Thurs, wifi

## Nez Perce County

*Getting Oriented*

Nez Perce county is on the West side of the state abutting Washington State. Lewiston is the largest city.

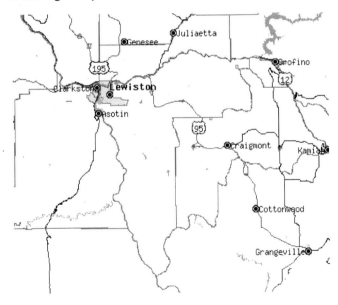

## Map of Lewiston Area
From Wikimedia Commons, PD USGov

**Lenore** GPS: 46.30N, 116.33 W ; Elevation: 945 feet, not much here

## Hells Canyon National Recreation Area

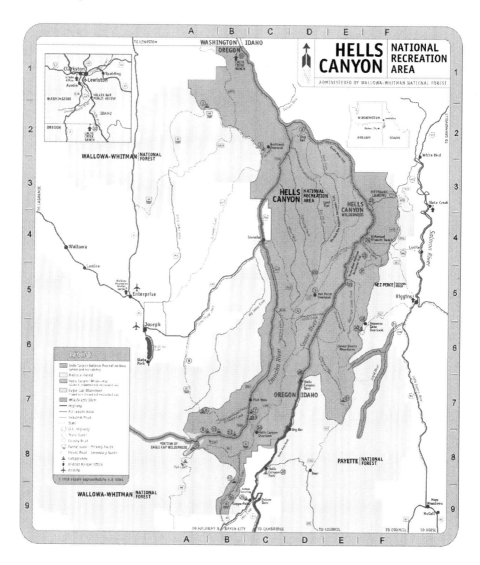

## Map of Hells Canyon

*Getting Oriented*

- Accessible from several areas. White Bird take FR 493 (Deer Creek Rd) W. From Lucile, take FR 242 W. From Riggins, take FR 241 and get to Snake River National Recreation Trail or FR 517 to Heavens Gate Overlook. See below

- Hell's Canyon is the deepest gorge in the United States at 8043ft deep. The Snake River winds through the canyon dividing the Wilderness area into two sides. The Idaho side ascends to the Seven Devils while the Oregon side gradually rises to ridges and meadows.

  *Media Connection: For a brochure and map on the Canyon, download here, http://www.fs.usda.gov/Internet/FSE_DOCUMENTS/stelprdb5411259.pdf*

## Practicalities

- Visitor Information

  Hells Canyon Creek Visitor Center, Idaho Power Rd to Hells Canyon Dam, 541-785-3395, 8am-4pm, vault toilets, interpretive signs, picnic area

## Activities

- Pittsburgh Landing, FR 493, off Hwy. 95 at White Bird to Old Hwy. 95 at MM 222 (sign to Pittsburg Landing and Hammer Creek Recreation Area) go about 1m over a bridge and turn on Deer Creek Rd (FR 493) for 16.5m to FR 493A and turn left 1.3m to parking area, accessible to most vehicles, restrooms, trail head

  Pittsburgh landing trail takes hikers 6m to Historic Kirkwood Ranch. Best in spring or fall.

Hells Canyon, wikipedia, X-Weinzar creative commons license

- Kirkwood Historic Ranch, off Hwy. 95 at Lucile to FR 242 for 16.5m

- Stud Creek Trail, starts at the Hells Canyon Creek Visitor Center, 1m down the river,

- Heavens Gate Overlook, very steep, rough and winding gravel road, FR 517 (seven Devils Rd), 19m

Incredible views and a great place for a picnic. To the south are the Seven Devils.

Heavens Gate Overlook, Wikimedia, Creative Commons, Dsdugan

## Spalding GPS: 46.26N, 116.49 W ; Elevation: 1278 feet

### Getting Oriented

- Off Hwy. 95

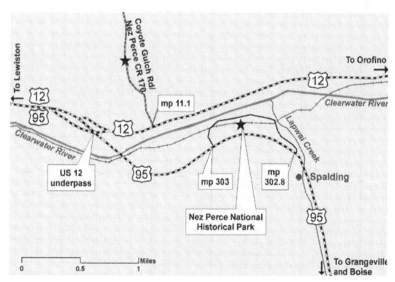

## Map of Hwy 12 and Spalding

(courtesy of fishandgame.idaho.gov)

*Practicalities*

- Weippe Public Library, 204 Wood St, 208-432-4058

*Activities*

- *Nez Perce National Historical Park Visitor Center, 39063 Hwy. 95, 208-843-7001, 8am-5pm, picnic tables, restrooms

    Museum exhibits and film as well as ranger led programs. Four short interpretive trails that combine for about 2.4m.

    *Media Connection: the National park Service has created a brochure with brief details about Nez Perce sites in the area, http://www.nps.gov/nepe/planyourvisit/upload/2008%20Lewis%20and%20Clark.pdf*

    *A Bird Guide is available here http://www.nps.gov/nepe/planyourvisit/upload/Bird-Guide_073012.pdf*

    *A Trail Map is available here, http://www.nps.gov/nepe/planyourvisit/upload/Draft_093010.pdf*

- White Bird Battlefield, 7m S of the Nez Perce Visitor Center, 1.5 RT, no facilities

    *media connection: download a brochure about the battlefield here, http://www.nps.gov/nepe/planyourvisit/upload/WHBI_Guide_WEB.pdf*

**Lewiston** GPS: 46.41N, 117.02 W ; Elevation: 745 feet

*Getting Oriented*

- Heads up: this valley can be very hot with temps in the 100's in July in August.

- Just to the S side of Hwy. 12 and S of Clearwater River on the border of Washington

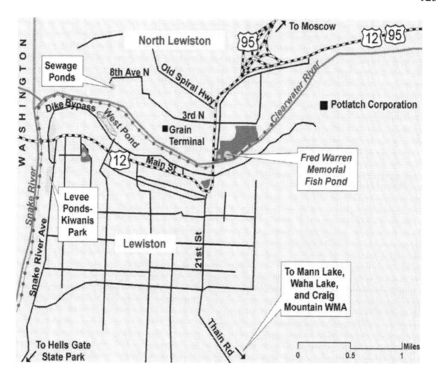

## Map of Lewiston
fishandgame.idaho.gov

*Practicalities*

- Visitor Information

  www.cityoflewiston.org

  beautifuldowntownlewiston.com

  Nez Perce Tribal Tourism, 17500 Nez Perce Rd, 208-298-1107, www.nezperce.org

- Library

  Lewiston City Library, 411 D St, 208-798-2525

- Laundromat

  Southway Dynamart, 822 16th Ave, 208-746-2227

- Grocery

Major Grocery stores throughout the city

*Events*
- Art Under the Elms, www.lcsc.edu/ce/aue/, late April

*Parks*
- Airport Park, 528 Cedar Ave, playground, playing fields

- Baughman Park, 102 Snake River Ave

- Brackenbury Square, 605 Main St

  located right downtown with lots of picnic tables, concerts in the summer on Saturday

- Clearwater Park, 3rd Ave N & 24th St, ball fields

- Community Park, 1239 Warner Ave, 2.5m walking paths, portable toilet, picnic tables

- Demolay park, 1402 Prospect Ave, park benches overlook the Snake River

- East End Boat Ramp, 3213 N & S Highway, Lewis-Clark memorial grove

- Fenton park, 716 13th St., playground

- Hathaway Field, 414 Bryden Ave, ball fields

- Hereth Park, 1534 powers Ave, playground, restrooms

- Jewett Park, 408 22nd Ave, playground

- Kiwanis Park and Mtn Dw Skate, playground, restrooms

- Lewiston Steelhead park, Located off Hwy. 95 at MM 311.74 on the frontage road, rest area, boat launch, restrooms

- Locomotive Park, 2102 Main St., picnic tables, locomotive and caboose

- Modie park, 1035 21st St., restrooms, butterfly garden, fitness path

- Pepsi Park, 2130 1st Ave N, play fields, restrooms, playground

- Pioneer Park, 203 5th St., playground

- Prospect Park, 814 Prospect Ave, benches to view the Snake River

- Rettig Square, 117 12th St.

- Rose Garden, 2031 N & S Highway

- Sunset Park, 2602 11th Ave., play fields, restrooms, playground

- Syringa Park, 3423 Syringa Dr., bathrooms, playground, walking trail

- Trevitt Park, 510 8th St.

- *Hells Gate State Park, 5100 Hells Gate Rd, 208-799-5187, fee, beach, picnic areas, small store, both the Jack O'Connor and Lewis and Clark Discovery Center are situated in the park (see below)

  Campsite has lots of trees and bushes and sites are "riverfront" but don't have much of a view. Trails include the Clearwater & Snake River National Recreation Trail, see below.

*Guides and Tours*

- Beamers Hells Canyon Tours, 1451 Bridge St, 509-758-4800, www.hellscanyontours.com, depart from Clarkson, $139 for half day tours, dinner cruise, wine tasting cruise, brunch cruise, fishing charters

- Historic Downtown Lewiston Walking Tour, self guiding brochure http://beautifuldowntownlewiston.org/Content/WalkingTourMap.pdf

- Idaho History Tours, 208-790-1257, idahohistorytours.com, 2hr, $19, 12 and older

  Ghost and walking tours as well as Trolley tours

- River Quest Excursions, 4203 Snake River Ave, 800-589-1129, www.riverquestexcursions.com, fishing, jet boat tours

- Snake River Adventures, 227 Snake River Ave, 800-262-8874, www.snakeriveradventures.com, jet boat tours, fishing, shuttles

*Byways*

- Northwest Passage Scenic Byway, travel on Hwy. 12 to the Idaho/Montana border,

  2 lane winding road parallels both the Lewis & Clark and Nez Perce Historic Trails passing through Spalding, Orofino, Kamiah, Grangeville to the Lolo Pass Visitor Center.

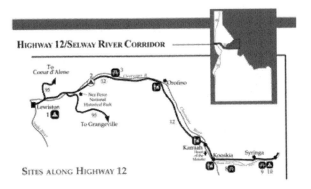

## Map of Hwy. 12

US Forest Service Map

*Cultural Attractions*

- Jack O'Connor Hunting Heritage & Education Center, 5600 Hells Gate Rd, 208-743-5043, www.jack-oconnor.org, 10-4pm, closed Mon.

  Writer and Hunter, O'Connor's center includes 65 mounted heads, photos and writings.

- *Lewis and Clark Discovery Center, 4832 Hells Gate Rd, 208-799-5015

  30 minute film and a variety of exhibits explain the Lewis and Clark expedition, particularly their struggle to cross the Rockies in Idaho. The museum itself is set on the Snake River in an attractive setting.

- *Lewis-Clark State College Center for Arts & History, 721 7th Ave, 208-792-2243, www.artsandhistory.org, 11-4 Tues-Sat

  Set in a building constructed in 1884 as the Vollmer Great Bargain Store, the 12,000 square exhibit space houses a variety of rotating art displays. Many exhibits showcase the history of Chinese miners in the 1860's.

- Nez Perce County Historical Museum, 306 3rd St, 208-743-2535, www.npchistsoc.org, 10-4pm Tues-Sat.

  The focus is the Nez Perce and Lewis and Clark but exhibits also display geology and river navigation. The building itself was once Lewiston's first hotel in 1862.

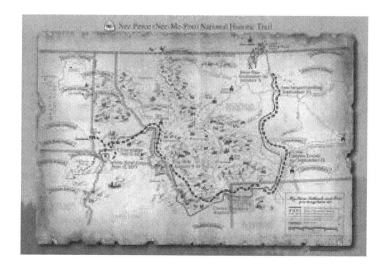

## Map of Nez Perce National Historic Trail

(Courtesy of the University of Texas Libraries, The University of Texas at Austin)

- Tsceminicum Sculpture, at the junction of the Snake and Clearwater River in Hells Gate Park near the Lewis and Clark Center,

  Bronze sculpture depicts the Nez Perce myths.

*Natural Attractions*

- Lewiston Wildlife Habitat Area, 10th St then Right on Warner Ave 1.5m,

  Trail and underwater viewing station as well as an observation gazebo.

  *Media Connection: Fish and Game created a brochure about the area that includes a map, http://fishandgame.idaho.gov/public/education/lwhaBrochure.pdf*

- Ant and Yellow Jacket, Hwy. 12 MM 10.9, pull off and interpretive sign of this basalt rock outcropping

  *Learn More About It: the name of this rock formation comes from a Nez Perce legend. Ant and Yellowjacket were arguing about who gets to sit on a rock to enjoy some Salmon. Coyote, the trickster of Native American stories, urges them to stop but when they don't, he turns them into rocks.*

*Activities*

- Clearwater River Casino & Resort, 17500 Nez Perce Rd, 208-298-1400, www.crcasino.com

- Hells Gate Marina and Restaurant, 4832 Hells Gate Marina, 208-799-5016, hellscanyon.net/Hells_Canyon_Hells_Gate_Marina.htm, convenient mart, kayak rental

## Biking

- Bike Lewiston Area information is available at www.twinriverscyclists.org

- Beautiful Downtown Lewiston website has a small collection of biking/walking routes in the city, http://www.beautifuldowntownlewiston.com/more/read-run-ride/

- Bike Rentals

  Pedals-N-Spokes, 829 D St, 208-743-6567

## Hiking

- Clearwater & Snake River National Recreation Trail, at N end of Hells Gate State Park, 1.8m trail in Lewiston but travels further S for a total of 18m

  *Media Connection: For an excellent brochure about the trail and parks along it, http://www.americantrails.org/NRTDatabase/trailPhotos/2372_Clearwaterand SnakeRiverNRT.pdf*

  Trail wanders along the river.

- Emerson Creek Campground, 16m south on County Rd 1/Surprise Valley Rd, turn right on County Rd 40 for 3miles, not recommended for trailers or large North Emerson Hiking Trail, 4.5m, steep trail

- Lewiston Levee Parkway Trail, multiple starting points, Hellsgate State Park, Steelgate Park, Locomotive Park, 35m loop

  Trail does not have much shade and runs down the Snake River, onto the Levee to the Lewis and Clark Center then up the Clearwater River to Locomotive Park. Continue to Memorial Bridge and then to Lower Goose Pasture for the entire loop

- Hells Gate State Park Trails, 5100 Hells Gate Rd, 208-799-5015, a variety of trails are accessible here

  Several miles of trails are available here with a couple of miles paved. You can start at the Lewis and Clark Discover Center and head either N or S. The S route has more trail options winding among the hills.

*Rafting*
- Snake River Adventures, 227 Snake River Ave, 800-262-8874, www.snakeriveradventures.com, jet boat tours, 1/2 day and full day tours, $110 adults for half day, $55 for children

*Wine, Beer and Cocktails*
- Clearwater Canyon Cellars, 1708 6th Ave, 208-816-4679, www.cccellars.com, 1-5pm Sat.

*Coffee*
- Blue Lantern Coffee House, 326 Main St, 208-413-6704, facebook page, 7am-5pm, occasional live music, pastries, beer and wine, wifi

  Attractive coffee shop with fun decor and comfortable seating, pastry and lunch offerings

- Coffee Cow, 1441 G St, 208-798-4488, 6am-6pm

- Greyson's Sandwich & Coffee House, 524 Main St, 208-743-0220, 8am-5pm

*Bakery and Treats*
- Bridge Baking, 607 7th Ave, 208-413-1460, bridgebaking.com, gluten free, delivery only

- Polar Bear Frozen Yogurt, 804 16th Ave, 208-746-1429, www.polarbearlewiston.com, 6am-9pm, sandwiches, espresso and yogurt

*Dining*
- Antonio's Pizza and Pasta, 1407 Main St, 208-746-6262, antonioslewiston.com, 11-9pm, under $20

  Large salad bar, pizza, pasta, steak and sandwiches, place has a huge menu.

- Bait Shop Grill, 3206 5th St, 208-746-1562, 7am-2pm

  Big, traditional American breakfasts

- Bojacks' Broiler Pit, 311 Main St, 208-743-9817, www.bojacksbroilerpit.com, 5pm-9:15pm

  Upon entering Bojack's, it feels like a step back to restaurants of old, nothing fancy just simple tablecloths, brick walls, heavy white plates, comfortable chairs and dark, dark, dark. Serves huge steak dinners that come with a side and salad. Don't be frightened by the outside or the bar you walk through to get to dinner. Steaks come highly recommended.

- Effie's Tavern, 1120 Main St, 208-746-1889

  Burgers and fries old-school neighborhood tavern. burgers are huge and not cheap ($10 and up).

- El Sombrero, 2215 Main Rd, 405 Thain Rd, 208-746-0658, elsombrero-fajita.com/lewiston-thain.htm, 11-10pm, under $15

  Brightly colored, lively Mexican with five locations and huge platters of food.

- Greyson's Sandwich & Coffee House, 524 Main St, 208-743-0220, 8am-5pm, still here?

  Spacious, comfortable coffee house with lots of light and attractive decor.

- Emperor of India-King Thai, 858 Main St, 208-798-0505, www.emperorofindiakingthai.com, beer and wine, 11-2 and 4-9, closed Mon., no credit cards

  Somewhat upscale setting with cloth table cloths and Asian-style decor. Daily specials. Menu is small with an emphasis on Chicken and fish. Owner runs everything so food can take time and options may be limited.

- *Hells Canyon Smokehouse, 145 Thain Rd, Suite K, 208-816-1709, facebook page, 11-8pm, take out with plans to expand

  BBQ with ribs, brisket and pork as well as a variety of sides mac and cheese, beans,

- Jollymore's, 1516 Main St, 208-743-9448, 11-10pm, wine and beer

  Upscale dining experience with a nice selection of interesting and traditional fare such as a pretzel BBQ sandwich or a steak, crab cakes or smoked mushroom chicken. Desserts are also worth a try including the pumpkin cheesecake or the chocolate cake.

- Lunch Box Deli, 602 20th St N, 208-743-5616, lunchboxdeliandbbq.com, 10:30 til the food runs out, most items under $10

  St Louis style ribs, pulled pork, smoked sausage or chicken served with beans, slaw, fries or soup. They also do Texas pit style bbq, salad, soup and burgers and deli style sandwiches.

- Main Street Grill, 625 Main St, 208-746-2440, mainstgrill.com, 10:30-8pm, chain

- MJ Barleyhoppers sports Bar and Brew Pub, 621 21st St at the Red Lion Hotel, 208-799-1000, www.redlionlewiston.com/mj_barleyhoppers.htm, 4-11pm

  Oldest Brewpub in the state with at least 7 different hand-crafted ales and 5 seasonals. Pool tables, dart games and a Juke box.

- Meriwether's Restaurant, 621 21st St at the Red Lion Hotel, 208-746-9390

  Typical casual hotel restaurant.

- Season's Bistro, 302 Main St, 208-798-4994, www.seasonsbistroandcatering.com, 11am-2pm, under $25

  Upscale entrees with fish, pasta, beef and chicken attractively plated. Contemporary decor with high ceilings, leather chairs and white table cloths.

- Sidelines Grill, 514 Main St, 208-790-0085, lewistonsidelinesgrille.com, 11am-2am, full bar, under $15

  Big time sports bar with a typical menu including sliders, nachos, burgers and wings.

- Southway Pizzeria & Deli, 721 Southway Ave, 208-743-0400, www.southwaypizzeria.com, delivery, 10:30-9:30, under $20, part of a chain

- Taco Cecy, 1350 Main St., 208-553-2600, delivery, under $10

  Restaurant is casual and serves authentic Mexican food. The hot sauces are green and red. Try both.

- Waffles & More, 1421 Main St, 208-743-5189, under $10

  Big, rich, sweet breakfasts like chocolate chip pancakes covered in strawberries and whipped cream, or smores waffles which is exactly what it sounds like, biscuits and gravy, or typical eggs and bagon. Also serves burgers, burritos, salads and sandwiches

- Waha Grill, 40787 Waha Rd, 208-746-7761, www.wahagrill.com, 12-8pm, under $15

  Burgers and fries, wings, hot dogs, pork tenderloin and all kinds of fried appetizers (very strong personal Christian message and boycot available on website)

- Zany Graze, 2004 19th Ave, 208-746-8131, www.zanygraze.com, 10:30-10pm

  A little bit of everything at this local chain (mex, sushi, steak, burgers)

*Camping*
- Hells Gate State Park, 5100 Hells Gate Rd, 208-799-5187, fee, beach, picnic areas, small store, pull thru sites, archery, both the Jack O'Connor and Lewis and Clark Discovery Center are situated in the park (see below)

  Campsite has lots of trees and bushes and sites are "riverfront" but don't have much of a view.

- McKay's Bend Recreation Site, 18m E of Hwy. 12 on MM 18, 15 sites, full hookup, water, flush toilets, picnic tables, fire rings, showers, fee

*Lodging*
- Most major chains are represented.

- Cedars Inn, 1716 Main St, 877-848-8526, www.cedarsinnlewiston.com, continental breakfast, outdoor pool, wifi, laundry, $50-70

  Typical motel with some really bad reviews . . .

- Italianna Inn, 2728 11th Ave, 877-550-2662, www.italiannainn.com, pool,

  Rooms are simple and breakfast is served

- Kirby Creek Lodge, 227 Snake River Ave, 80miles upriver from Lewiston, 200-262-8874, www.snakeriveradventures.com, rates start at $125pp with your own transportation, $242pp for transport from Pittsburg landing, all meals available.

## Lapwai GPS: 46.24N, 116.48 W ; Elevation: 955 feet

*Getting Oriented*
- Hwy. 95 runs to the East of the small town

*Practicalities*
- Grocery

  Valley Foods, 204N Hwy. 95, 208-843-2070, full service grocery with deli

*Activities*
- City Park, 315 S Main St., playground, picnic tables, seasonal restrooms

*Dining*
- Donald's Family Dining, 304 N hwy. 95, 208-843-7273, 6am-8pm

  Burgers, sandwiches, full breakfasts

## Sweetwater GPS: 46.22N, 116.47 W ; Elevation: 1096 ft, not much here

## Culdesac GPS: 46.22N, 116.40 W ; Elevation: 1644 feet

*Getting Oriented*
- Located just N of Hwy. 95

*Practicalities*
- Library

  Culdesac City Library, 714 Main St, 208-843-5215

*Dining*
- Drovers Run at Jacques Spur, 49038 Hwy. 95, 208-843-9162, facebook page with updates, under construction and opening soon

## Gifford GPS: 46.26N, 116.33 ; Elevation 2949 ft, nothing here

## Lemhi County

*Getting Oriented*
- Located in Eastern Idaho, Salmon is the largest town.

*Practicalities*
- Visitor Information

  lemhicountyidaho.org

## North Fork GPS: 45.24N, 113.59W ; Elevation: 3620ft

*Getting Oriented*
- Hwy. 93, 25m from Salmon Idaho

*Practicalities*
- Visitor Information

  thevillageatnorthfork.com

  North Fork Ranger District, 11 Casey Rd, 208-865-2700, 8am-4:30 Mon-Fri.

- Grocery

  North Fork Store, 2046 Hwy. 93, 208-865-7001, groceries and sundries, gas, outdoor supplies, fish and game licenses

*Activities*
- North Fork Guides, 208-865-2534, www.northforkguides.com, whitewater rafting, fishing

*Dining*

- Josephine's RV Park and Campground Pizza, 2570 Hwy. 93N, 208-514-6986, www.josephinesidahorvpark.com, 5-9pm, Thurs-Sun dine in, Weds take out, wine and beer, under $25

  Park is located on the river with great views and frequent wildlife sightings

- The Village at North Fork Cafe, 2046 Hwy. 93N, 208-865-7001, thevillageatnorthfork.com, seasonal

  Traditional American food meals like chicken fried steak, fish and chips, burgers

*Camping*

- Josephine's RV Park and Campground, 2570 Hwy. 93N, 208-514-6986, www.josephinesidahorvpark.com, full hook ups, potable water, wifi, picnic tables, restrooms, coin operated showers

- Wagonhammer RV Park & Campground, 1826 Hwy. 93, 208-865-2477, 928-855-1899, wagonhammercampground.com, wifi, full hookups, pull thru, restrooms, showers, recreation room, laundry, convenient mart, fishing, picnic tables, pet friendly

  Campground is by the river

*Lodging*

- Rivers Fork, 2036 hwy. 93N, 208-865-2301, www.riversfork.com, wifi

  Basic, comfortable rooms with great views sitting right on the Salmon river

- The Village at North Fork, 2046 Hwy. 93N, 208-865-7001, thevillageatnorthfork.com, 7 rooms, wifi, air con, laundry, $79 includes dinner in the cafe

  Rooms are simple with iron bedsteads and big fluffy duvets and include room for at least four.

## Shoup GPS 45.22N, 114.16 W ; Elevation: 3389 feet

*Getting Oriented*

- On Salmon River Rd right along the Salmon River. A ghost town, mostly, the town still offers limited services for recreation.

*Activities*

- Booker's Retreat and Mother Chukar's Cafe, 2660 Salmon Rd, 208-394-2130, www.bookersretreat.com. Boat rentals for paddle rafts and kayaks with delivery

*Dining*

- Booker's Retreat and Mother Chukar's Cafe, 2660 Salmon Rd, 208-394-2130, www.bookersretreat.com, almost everything is under $20, beer and wine

  Full breakfast, lots of snack options, sandwiches, burgers and salads as well as steaks

*Lodging*

- Booker's Retreat and Mother Chukar's Cafe, 2660 Salmon Rd, 208-394-2130, www.bookersretreat.com, rustic campground and cabins with limited services (no running water, no electricity, but propane heat and gas lanterns), restrooms are in shower building, $30-70

  The place is off the grid so there are no hook ups or water at the campground but water can be filled at the cafe.

## Carmen GPS: 45.14N, 113.53 W ; Elevation: 3825 feet, not much here

*Learn More About It: The Frank Church River of No Return Wilderness Area (referred to as "The Frank" is the second largest wilderness are in the lower 48. It is completely contained in Idaho and takes up much of the central region of the state encompassing over 2 million acres. The Middle Fork of the Salmon carves its way through a deep, 6300 ft, canyon (deeper than the Grand Canyon) and has been dubbed "the river of no return". The Salmon River Mountains run through the center of the wilderness with multiple lakes and great forests. 2600 miles of trails crisscross the area but it still remains largely undeveloped and undisturbed (except for logging).*

*Getting Oriented*

- On Hwy. 93

*Activities*

- Frank Church Wilderness, very rustic wilderness

  For extensive information,
  http://www.fs.usda.gov/Internet/FSE_DOCUMENTS/stelprd3792566.pdf

  http://www.fs.usda.gov/Internet/FSE_DOCUMENTS/stelprd3792564.pdf

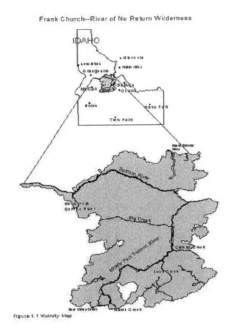

Figure 1.1 Vicinity Map

## Map of River of No Return Wilderness

(From Wikipedia.org, courtesy of US Forest Service, Image is in the public domain)

- Warren River Expeditions, 15 ed Tail Lane, 208-756-6387, www.raftidaho.com, fishing, rafting

**Salmon** GPS: 45.10N, 113.54W ; Elevation: 3944ft

*Getting Oriented*
- Hwy 93 runs right through Salmon. The Salmon River divides the town.

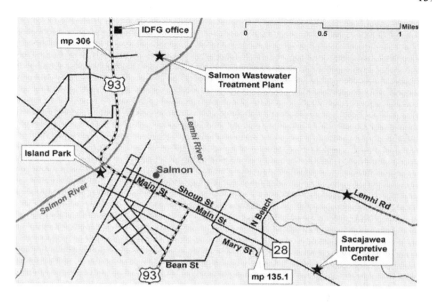

## Map of Salmon

fishandgame.idaho.gov

*Practicalities*

- Visitor Information

  Eastern Idaho BLM Salmon Field Office, 1206 South Challis, 208-756-5400

  Salmon Region Fish and Game, 99 Hwy. 93N, 208-756-2271

  Salmon Valley Chamber of Commerce, 200 Mail St, 800-727-2540, www.salmonchamber.com

  www.cityofsalmon.com

- Grocery

  Corner Store, 410 Courthouse Dr, 208-756-2113

  Saveway Market, 1200 Shoup St, 208-756-2822, 7am-9pm, closed Sun, full service grocery with

- Laundry

  Salmon River RV Park Cafe, 111 Whitetail Dr, 20m S of Salmon on Hwy. 93, 208-756-4565, www.salmonriverrvp.com

  Service Grocery & Laundromat, 519 Union Ave, 208-756-2832

- Library

  Salmon Public Library, 204 S Main St, 208-756-2311, salmonlibrary.org

## Guides and Tours

- 100 Acre Wood Resort, 2356 Hwy 93, www.100acrewoodlodge.com, 208-865-2165

  Variety of guided tours including float trips, fishing, hiking, bear viewing and horseback riding

- See additional tour information under Rafting

## Activities

- Lemhi County Historical Society, 210 Main St, 208-756-3342, www.lemhicountymuseum.org, fee, seasonal

- Tower Creek Pirimids day use site, Carmen Creek Rd, off Hwy. 93 E, picnic tables, homesteader's cabin, interpretive panels

  *Media Connection: The Forest Service has put together a brochure explaining the history and flora and fauna of the site. Download it here: http://www.fs.fed.us/outdoors/naturewatch/implementation/Marketing/Interpretive-Placemats.pdf*

- Tower Rock Recreation Site, Hwy. 93 10 m, 6 sites, restrooms, no drinking water, picnic area, fishing

- Sacagawea Interpretive Center, Lewis and Clark St, Hwy. 28, 208-756-1188, www.sacajaweacenter.org, 8am-2pm learning center, 9am-5pm Visitor Center.

  71 acre grounds include a Heritage Garden, a visitor center and regular interpretive events.

## Biking

- http://idaholosttrails.blogspot.com/

- www.ridesalmon.com

- Continental Divide Trail, over 100 miles of the 3000 mile long trail are accessible near Salmon, many off of Hwy. 28 or Hwy. 93, www.continentaldividetrail.org/.

  The continental divide trail runs along the border of Idaho and Montana

- Wagonhammer Trail System, 20m N of Salmon on Hwy. 93 to FR 72, idaholosttrails.blogspot.com/p/wgonhammer.html

*Horseback Riding*

- Geertson Creek Trail Rides, 151 Geertson Creek Rd, 208-756-2463, geertson.com

- Rawhide Outfitters, 204 Larson St, 208-756-4276, rawhideoutfitters.com, white water rafting, float trips, fishing, horseback riding, Lewis and Clark tours

*Hiking*

- Nez Perce National Historic Trail, couldn't find info, maybe not a hiking trail?

- Gold bug Hot Springs, MM 282, 2.5m one way to undeveloped springs

- Lewis and Clark Discovery Trail, to Burns Gulch, idaholosttrails.blogspot.com/p/wgonhammer.html, begins at Burns Gulch Trailhead and ends at Trail Creek Trailhead, 9.1m

- *Discovery Hill, St Charles Street N for 2m when it turns to gravel continue and the trailhead is just ahead.

  Motorized and non-motorized trails. The Podcast trail is a 1.6m trail with podcasts about the scenery and surrounds.

*Rafting and Fishing*

- Arctic Creek Lodge and Tours, 22 Hammon Dr, 208-756-1657, www.arcticcreeklodge.com, jet boat shuttles, scenic tours, fishing

- Blackadar Boating, Hwy. 93 N, 208-756-3958, blackadarboating.com, raft rental, shuttle service

- Idaho Adventures, 208-756-1986, www.idahoadventures.com, rafting and floating trips, rentals of paddle boat, ore rafts, kayaks, paddle boards, shuttle service

- Salmon River Tours and China Bar Lodge, www.salmonrivertours.com, scenic tours, jetboat shuttle service, fishing

- Silver Cloud Expeditions, 208-756-6215, www.silvercloudexp.com, 1/2 day summer floats

*Scenic Drives*

- Hwy. 28 from Salmon to Tendoy (see below), 20 miles

  This route has Lewis and Clark interpretive signs

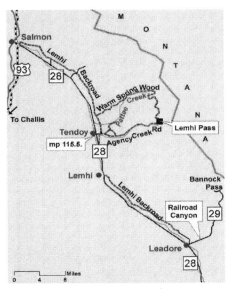

## Map of Salmon to Leadore,
(courtesy of fishandgame.idaho.gov)

- Sacajawea Historic Byway, Hwy,. 28 to Hwy. 33 to I15 (near Idaho Falls)

  The byway climbs to 7186 ft on a two lane road. Sacajawea known most famously for helping Lewis and Clark, was born in the Lemhi Valley where she lived until she was 12. She was captured by the Arikira Indians and lived with them in North Dakota until she joined the Crops of Discovery and returned to her native lands with them.

*Dining*

- *Bertram's Salmon Valley Brewery, 101 S Andrews, 208-756-3391, bertramsbrewery.com, under $20

  Traditional pub grub but also more substantial entrees. There are brats, chili and hot dogs but burgers, steak sandwiches and pasta and salmon can be ordered at dinner. Decor is decidedly casual

- Cowboy Grill, 519 Main St, 208-756-2228, 11-4pm, www.reddogdiner.net, under $10

  Charbroiled burgers and chicken with fresh cut fries. Hard ice cream for dessert.

- Dave's Pizza, 2011 Main St, 208-756-4565, davespizzarestaurant.com, 11-9pm,

  Soup, wings and pizza

- Oddfellows Bakery, 510 Main St, 208-756-1122, 7am-5pm, closed sun.

Coffee and baked goods including fresh baked bread in a wood fired oven for lunch sandwiches. Serves House Roasted Coffee

- *Junkyard Bistro, 405 Main St, 208-756-3391, facebook page updated regularly, 11am-10pm, beer and wine, under $10

  Italian sandwiches, sushi and tapas and multiple vegetarian options served in an old tavern type atmosphere, more of a bar then trendy restaurant. Mushroom soup is very good. Burgers and Gyros served with salad for lunch food.

- Last Chance Pizza, 611 Lena St, 208-756-4559, 11am-10pm, evening delivery

- Red Dog Diner, 1200 Main St, 208-756-6555, reddogdiner.net, 8am-11am, under $10

  Breakfast is traditional favorites with a few Mexican options.

- Salmon River Coffee Shop, 606 Main St, 208-756-3521

  Traditional, American Favorites in a diner style atmosphere

- Salmon River RV Park Cafe, 111 Whitetail Dr, 20m S of Salmon on Hwy. 93, 208-756-4565, www.salmonriverrvp.com, 8am-2pm, Weds-Sun, home baked goodies, might be closed

  Rustic country cafe atmosphere with a traditional American menu with specials throughout the month

- The Savage Grill, 907 Mulkey St, 208-756-2062, facebook page, 11am-7pm, delivery

  Burgers and fries in a small, casual eatery. Some of the decor might be considered offensive . . . Ice cream.

- The Shady Nook, 501 River Front Dr, 2 blocks N on hwy. 93, 208-756-4182, ww.theshadynook.com, 4-10:30, closed Sun, beer and wine, under $25

  Lounge features televisions for sports viewing while the restaurant is family friendly. Almost everything is prepared in house with fresh ingredients. Menu features an eclectic blend of regional cuisine (like smoked trout), healthy fare (steamed Edamame) and traditional favorites (Nachos, beer battered veggies). Entrees are heavy on fish and beef

## Camping

- Century II Campground, 603 Riverfront Dr, 208-756-2063, century2campground.com, cabins, wifi, restrooms and showers, laundry

Located on the banks of the Salmon River

- Fort Limhi Trading Post & RV Park, 3 Bennett Ln, East of town on Hwy. 28, 208-756-1330, salmondidaho.com

- Heald's Haven RV Park, 22 Heald Haven Dr, 12m S of Salmon on Hwy. 93, 208-756-3629, www.healdshaven.com, pull thru, restrooms, fire rings, picnic tables,

- Royal Gorge Resort, 3689 Hwy. 93, 208-876-4130, www.royalgorgeresort.com, rustic cabins ($50-90), wifi, dumping, fire pit, restrooms, showers, boat launch, playground, full hookups, fishing

A mile of riverfront

- Salmon River RV Park & Cafe, 111 Whitetail Dr, 20m S of Salmon on Hwy. 93, 208-756-4565, www.salmonriverrvp.com, 20 sites, hook ups, fishing, hot springs, small store and cafe, laundry

- Shoup Bridge Recreation Site, Hwy. 93 S of Salmon, 5 sites, boat ramp, drinking water, restrooms, seasonal

- Tower Rock Recreation Site, Hwy. 93N 10 miles, 6 sites, fee, restrooms, picnic, no drinking water

- Wagonhammer Campground, 1826 Hwy. 93, 208-885-2477, wagonhammercampground.com, 52 sites, pull thru, full hook ups, water, showers, picnic table, gift shop, pet friendly

On the Salmon River, some sites literally abut the river while others are a short walk away. Trees and grass make for a green, shady setting.

- Williams Lake Campground, 5m S on Hwy. 93, 5200ft elevation, turn right at the Shoup Bridge and go 8m, vault toilets, boat ramp, fishing

## Lodging
- Arctic Creek Lodge & Tours, 22 Hammon Dr, 208-756-1657, articcreeklodge.com

Simple, rustic lodge

- Bear Country Inn, 1015 Main St, 208-756-1499, www.bearcountryinnsalmon.com, indoor pool, hot tub, laundry, wifi, pet friendly, $55-65

Basic motel rooms

- Greyhouse Inn, 1115 Hwy. 93S, 800-348-8097, www.grehhouseinn.com, full breakfast served, $92-124, some private and shared baths, inn and historic cabins, fishing trips offered

  Decor is a mixture of antique and eclectic (with lots and lots of red) in the Victorian Inn while the rustic cabins have full amenities including kitchens. Living room and decks for guest use.

- Sacajawea Inn, 705 S Challis, 208-756-2294, hotelsalmon.com, wifi, $53-$70, RV hook up available, fire pit, laundry

  Small motel but with an interesting decor, murals on the wall and wood floors. Breakfast is available for a small fee.

- Salmon River Motel, 104 Courthouse Dr, 208-756-8880, salmonmotel.com, wifi, air con, chain?

  Standard motel rooms

- Solaas Bed and Breakfast, 3 S Baker Rd, 9m SE on Hwy. 28, 888-425-5474, solaasbnb.com, $45-65

  Historic home constructed in 1905 serves a full breakfast with fresh fruit and veggies from the garden. Back patio for dining.

- Stagecoach Inn, 201 Riverfront Dr, 208-756-2294, stagecoachiinnmotel.com, wifi, free breakfast, hot tub, outdoor pool, laundry

  Standard motel rooms and suites with flat screen tv

- Syringa Lodge, 13 Gott Lane, 877-580-6482, syringalodge.com, 6 rooms, $80-140, includes full breakfast, wifi

  The recently renovated Lodge, built of Spruce logs, sits above the town, overlooking the Salmon River and the mountains in the distance. Rooms have Western decor, wood floors and hewn log walls.

- Wagon West Motel, 503 Hwy. 93N, 208-756-4281, wagonswestmotel.com, fire pit, rooms and family suites, $40-70, basic motel rooms some with kitchens

- 100 Acre Wood Resort, www.100acrewoodlodge.com, 208-865-2165, complimentary hot breakfast, hot tub, paddle boats, air con, wifi, fishing, $70-130, dinners are served to guests

  Suites and rooms are decorated with lodge pole pine, clean, bright colors and lots of windows. Jacuzzi tubs and fireplaces are also available. Lodge rooms share a bath.

# Tendoy GPS: 44.57N, 113.38W ; Elevation: 4842 ft.

*Learn More About It: Tendoy was the name of the Lemhi Shoshone Chief from 1863-1907. A peaceful chief, he both resisted pressure to move his tribe to an area near Pocatello Idaho but also got along with the local settlers.*

## Getting Oriented
- Hwy. 28 E of Hwy. 93

## Practicalities
- Visitor Information

  Sula Ranger Station, 7383 Hwy. 93, MM 11 Hwy. 93, in Montana, 406-821-3201

  www.leadorechamber.com

- Grocery

  Tendoy Store & Wine Tasting Room, 1944 Hwy. 28, 208-756-2263

## Activities
- Lemhi Pass trail, gravel Agency Creek Rd, 12m E of Tendoy off old Hwy. 28, parking, interpretive signs, picnic tables, vault toilets, hiking trails, some steep sections on the road

  Access to Lewis & Clark National Historic Trail, Continental Divide Scenic Trail and Laura Tolman Scott Wildflower Trail

  *Media Connection: Forest Service has a brochure about Lemhi Pass, http://www.fs.usda.gov/Internet/FSE_DOCUMENTS/stelprdb5052332.pdf*

- Lost Trail Powder Mountain, Hwy. 93 S St, Sula MT, 406-821-3211, at the Montana/Idaho border, Thurs-Sun, ski and snowboard lessons and rentals, cafe on site

- Sharkey Hot Springs, Old Hwy. 28 (Warm Springs Rd) MM 4.8, outdoor soaking pools, changing rooms, vault toilets, picnic tables, fee

- Lewis & Clark Back Country Byway, Hwy. 28 in Tendoy idaho to Old Hwy 28 (the Lemhi back road to the Warm Spring Wood Road), 39 miles, vault toilets and picnic tables on the way

  Single lane gravel road loop that climbs 3000 ft with a grade that can exceed 5%. There are interpretive signs along the route explaining Lewis and Clark stops. The road is passable by passenger car with good tires.

*Media Connection: the BLM has written a brochure about this route. Access it here:*
*http://www.blm.gov/pgdata/etc/medialib/blm/id/special_areas/byways___tra*
*ils/lewis_and_clark_backcounty.Par.84759.File.dat/LCBackCountryByway_web.*
*pdf*

## Camping

- Agency Creek Campground, 4m E on Old Hwy. 28 on Agency Creek Rd, 4 sites, restrooms

## Leadore GPS: 44.40N, 113.21W ; Elevation 5971 ft

### Getting Oriented

- Hwy. 28 runs through Leadore (and is Railroad St in town) and intersects with Hwy. 29 which heads off East.

  *Media Connection: The Forest Service created a brochure for a Nez Perce drive from Leadore to Snowline Mt. It can be accessed here,*
  *http://www.fs.usda.gov/Internet/FSE_DOCUMENTS/fsbdev3_055553.pdf*

### Practicalities

- Visitor Information

  Leadore Ranger Station, 176 S Railroad St, 208-768-2500

- Grocery

  Stage Stop Junction, 100 Railroad Ave, 208-768-2313, convenience store and deli

- Library

  Leadore Community Library, 202 S Railroad St, 208-768-2640, leadore.lili.org, wifi (accessible even when library isn' t open).

### Activities

- Leadore City Park and Rodeo Grounds, Hwy. 28 N of town, free camping

- Meadow Lake Interpretive Trail, 17m S on Hwy. 28 and go W on gravel FR 002, climbing 2000 ft to the campground, .9m trail and 1.2m trail available

### Dining

- Silver Dollar Restaurant & Bar, 205 S Railroad St, 208-768-2688, 8am-8pm

- Stage Stop Junction, 100 Railroad Ave, 208-768-2313, convenience store and deli

*Camping*

- Lema's RV Park, 304 S Railroad St, 208-768-2030, 10 sites, drinking water, dump station, full hookups, pull thru

- Meadow Lake Campground, 17m S on Hwy. 28 and go W on gravel FR 002, climbing 2000 ft to the campground, 18 sites, potable water, vault toilet, picnic tables, fire rings, fishing, day hiking

*Lodging*

- Homestead Motel, 187 N Railroad St, Hwy. 28, 208-768-2742

- Leadore Inn, 401 S Railroad St, 208-768-2237, wifi

# Gibbonsville GPS: 45.33N, 113.55W ; Elevation: 4570 ft

*Getting Oriented*

- Forest Rd 079 turns off Hwy. 93 to the East to Gibbsonville

*Activities*

- Continental Divide Outfitters, 208-865-2665, www.continental-divide.com, full service hunting guides

- Keating Outfitters, 40 Dahlonega Creek Rd, 208-865-2252, www.21a-idaho-outfitters.com, hunting guides

*Dining*

- The Broken Arrow Restaurant, 3148 Hwy. 93N, 208-865-2241, thebrokenarrow.com, 5-9pm, occasional live music, indoor and outdoor seating

  Mexican and American food in a small, comfortable restaurant.

*Lodging*

- The Broken Arrow, 208-865-2241, thebrokenarrow.com, fishing, 6 cabins with shared baths, wifi, camping available, $32

  The North Fork of the Salmon runs behind the resort. CAbins are simple and dark.

# Custer County

*Getting Oriented*

- In the center of the state, Custer County includes the intersection of Hwy. 75 and 93 and the towns of Challis, Clayton and Salmon, the largest.

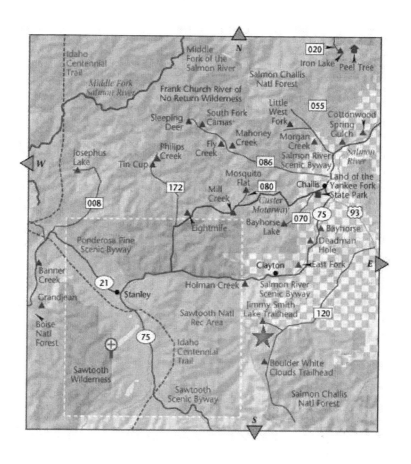

## Map of Sawtooth National Recreation Area
courtesy of blm.gov

*Practicalities*

- Visitor Information

  www.stanleycc.org

**Stanley** GPS: 44.12N, 114. 56 W ; Elevation: 6253 ft.

*Getting Oriented*

- Hwy. 75 runs to the East of the town, along the Salmon River. Most Services are off Hwy. 21 with a second small town a bit further N on Hwy. 75

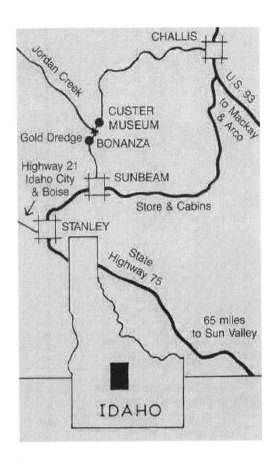

## Map of Stanley

(courtesy of fs.usda.gov)

### *Practicalities*

- Visitor Information

www.stanleycc.org

Stanley Ranger Station, 3m S on Hwy. 75 MM 186-187, 208-774-3000

Excellent source for information about the Sawtooth Wilderness

USFS Redfish Lake Visitor Center, on FR 214 off Hwy. 75, tours, campfire programs

- Grocery

Jerry's Country Store, 55 Lower Stanley, 208-774-3566, lowerstanley.com

Mountain Village Mercantile, 5 Eva Falls Ave, 208-774-3500, mountainvillage.com, full service grocery including liquor

- Library

Stanley Community Library, 33 Ace of Diamonds St, 208-774-2470, ruralnetwork.net/~stanlib, 12-4, wifi

*Byways*

- Ponderosa Pine Scenic Byway, Hwy. 21 runs from Boise North to Idaho City and up to Stanley

Road is paved but narrow and winding as it rises toward Stanley. Can be closed in winter

- Salmon River Scenic Byway, begins at the Montana border (elevation 6995 ft) at Lost Trail Pass and runs through Salmon to Stanley Idaho, 167m

Interpretive signs explain Lewis & Clark's travel through the area. Road passes through Salmon, Challis, Land of the Yankee Fork/Sunbeam and then to Stanley

> Day Trip: Traverse Hwy. 75 from Hwy. 93 W to Stanley and then to Galena Lodge (mileage is either N or S of Stanley)
>
> Land of the Yankee Fork State Park, junction of Hwy. 93 and 75
> Yankee Fork Ranger Station ?
> Holman Creek Campground, 25.5m N
> Torreys Hole Rec Site, 22m N
> Snyder Springs picnic area, vault toilet,
> Indian Riffles Overlook, 15.8m N
> Lower and Upper O'Brien, vault toilets, picnic tables, 15m N
> Elk Creek Boat Access, 14m N
> Sunbeam Dam, 13m N
> Custer Motorway/Custer Museum/Boot Hill Cemetery, 13m N to turnoff
> Sunbeam Hot Springs, 12.1m N, cafe and campground
> Basin Creek Hot Springs, 8.3m N
> Mormon Bend Campground
> Riverside Campground
> Boat Box Hot Springs, 3.3m N
> Joe's Gulch, 2.4m N
> Nip and Tuck Rd, 1.3m
> Stanley Museum, .6m N
> Stanley Ranger Station, 2.6m S
> Little Redfish Lake/Redfish Lake, 4.3m S

Redfish Center & Gallery, 5m S
Sawtooth Fish Hatchery, 5.9m S
Decker Flats, 15.3m S
Petit Lake, 18.1m S
Alturas Lake, 21m S

## Arts and Culture

- Custer Historic Mining Town, 13m N of Stanley on Hwy, 75 then 9m N on Yankee Fork Rd, seasonal, 10-6pm

- Custer Museum, ghost town and museum

- Redfish Center & Gallery, 5m S of Stanley on hwy. 75, W of Redfish Lake Lodge, 208-774-3376, opens Mid June, 9-4:30, free, nature hikes, educational programs, boat tours, wifi (access even when the center is closed), art gallery,

- Sawtooth Forum and Lecture Series, Fridays in July and August at Stanley Museum and Redfish Center

- *Stanley Historical Museum, Hwy. 75 MM 190, 208-774-3517, 11-5 seasonal, free, schedule a walking tour

  The museum is located in a historic Ranger Station and has exhibits on history of the Sawtooth Valley. Junior ranger programs are offered on Fri and Sat afternoons. Lectures on Fridays

## Biking

- Information

  adventurecycling.org

  *Media Connection: Lots of options for getting good maps for biking. There is a Stanley Trail app available in itunes (Stanley Trails). An excellent waterproof folded map is available at Adventuremaps.net, "Sawtooth/Whiteclouds, Idaho Trail Map & Guide"*

- Elk Meadows Loop Trail, 5m W of Stanley take Stanley Lake Rd 2.3m

- Fisher William (Fisher Creek), park at Williams Creek Trailhead, ride counter clockwise

- Basin Butte Lookout, W of Stanley Hwy. 21 5m and turn N on Stanley Creek Rd for 1.4m to Kelly Creek and turn left 10 m on winding dirt road

- Nip and Tuck, just N of Stanley, this road climbs 300ft to the summit with lots of ride options

- Trail from Stanley City Park to Redfish Lake, in progress

- Sawtooth Adventure Company, 866-774-4644, sawtoothadventure.com, guided mountain biking

- Rentals

  River Wear, Hwy. 21, 208-774-3591

  Redfish Lake Lodge, 208-774-3536

## *Hiking*

- Alpine Lake, 2.5m W of Stanley on Hwy. 21 follow Iron Creek Rd 3.2m to trailhead, 4m to lake with 1000ft climb

- Decker Flats, 15.3m S on Hwy. 75, turn W on dirt road, many trail options

  Hell Roaring, 5m to Lake with 600 ft elevation gain. Trail winds along Hell Roaring Creek. Interpretive panels at site.

- *Goat Lake, 6.8m RT, 1000 ft elevation gain with mostly shade. At 1.1m is a signed junction where those seeking a short hike can turn around. Requires a creek crossing with log. A falls is located behind the lake but scrambling is required

- Redfish Lake Loop, start near the lodge, 13.9m loop with climbing

- Sawtooth Lake, 2.5m W of Stanley follow Iron Creek Rd 3.2m to trailhead, 5m to lake with 1000ft climb, picnic tables, vault toilets

- Stanley Lake, paved Stanley Lake Rd W on Hwy. 21, trails

*Media Connection: The book "The Day Hiker's Guide to Stanley Idaho" by Scott Marchant is a useful book if you plan on hiking in this area.*

Stanley Lake and the Sawtooths

*Horseback Riding*
- Mystic Saddle Ranch, Fisher Creek Rd, 208-774-3591, mysticsaddleranch.com, day rides in Stanley and Redfish Lake

*Rafting and Fishing*
- Fly fishing report, flyfishingstanleyidaho.com

- Rentals

  Redfish Lake Lodge

  River Wear, Hwy. 21, 208-774-3592

  The River Company, 1150 Eva Falls Ave, 208-774-2244, www.therivercompany.com

  Riverside Motel and Sawtooth Rentals, 560 Mcgowan Ave, 208-774-3409

- The River Company, 1150 Eva Falls Ave, 800-398-0346, www.therivercompany.com, half day and lunch trips, fishing, $75 adult for half day

  Rapids are Class 2 and 3

- Salmon River Anglers/Sawtooth Adventure Company, Hwy. 75, 208-721-8772, fly fishing trips, rafting,

- Silver Creek Outfitters, 208-726-5282, silver-creek.com/fishing, provides guided fishing trips

- White Cloud Rafting Adventures, 635 Edna McGowen, 800-571-7238, www.whitecloudrafting.com, lunch trips, fishing, kayaking

*Activities*
- Alturas Lake, 21m S on hwy. 75 then W 1.8m on paved Rd, fishing, boating, hiking, several campgrounds

- Basin Creek Hot Springs, 8.3m N on Hwy. 75 MM 197 and 198, unimproved natural hot springs

  Water flows into these pools at 170 degrees.

- Boot Hill Cemetery, 13m N of Stanley on Hwy, 75 then 9m N on Yankee Fork Rd

  Old Cemetery

- Cape Horn Guard Station Loop, 11.4m W of Stanley, turn N off Hwy. 21 at Cape Horn Guard Station Sign, 7.3m dirt road loop with great wildlife viewing

- Historic Custer, Hwy. 75 to Yankee Fork Rd N, ghost town

  Town was established in 1879 to serve miners and declined as mines played out becoming a ghost town in 1910.

 Empire Saloon, Custer

Courtesy of Wikipedia.org, creative commons, Shelleylyn

- Indian Riffles Overlook, 16m N on Hwy. 75 MM 205-206, good viewing of traditional Salmon spawning beds

- Kelly Creek Rd, 5m W of Stanley turn N on Stanley Creek Rd 1.4m and then left to Basin Butte Lookout and turn Rt. Great wildlife viewing.

- Little Redfish Lake, 4.3m S on Hwy. 75, then .2m on paved rd.

- Music from Stanley, Redfish Lake Lodge, concert series on Sunday afternoons 4-7pm June-Sept

- Mystic Saddle Ranch, Fisher Creek Rd, mysticsaddleranch.com, 208-774-3591, 8am-5pm, horseback riding, fishing, hunting, wagon rides, cookouts

  Trail rides are offered at Redfish Corrals at Redfish Lake and Mystic Saddle Ranch

- Park Creek Nordic Trails, off Hwy. 21, 16km of trails, vault toilets

  *Media Connection: For a map of the ski trails, go here*
  *http://www.stanleycc.org/downloads/map-winter-parkcreek.pdf*

- Sawtooth Adventure Company, 67 Hwy. 75, 208-721-8772, sawtoothadventure.com, rafting, kayaking, fishing, mountain biking, paddle

- Sawtooth Fish Hatchery, 5.8m S on Hwy. 75 MM 183-184, 208-774-3684, 8am-5pm, three tours daily

*media connection: a virtual tour is available at the imnh.isu.edu website,*
*http://imnh.isu.edu/digitalatlas/geog/fishery/hatchery/sawtooth.htm*

- Sawtooth Mountain Guides, Nip and Tuck Rd, MP 125.9 on Hwy. 93, 208-774-3324, sawtoothguides.com, rock climbing guides, rock climbing classes, day hiking, fishing, rafting

- Stanley Creek Wildlife Area, MP 125.7, short interpretive trail with views of the Stanley Basin

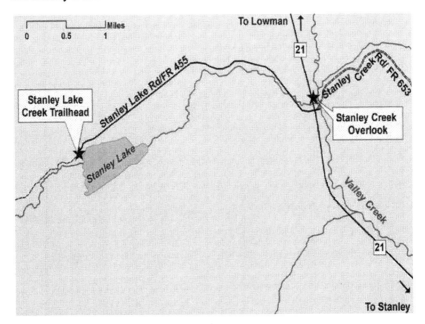

## Map of Hwy 21 and Stanley Lake
fishandgame.idaho.gov

- Stanley Idaho Disk Golf, Stanley City Park

- Stanley City Park, Hwy. 21, 2K groomed nordic ski trail,

- Stanley Lake, paved Stanley Lake Rd W on Hwy. 21, trails

- Sunbeam Hot Springs, 12m N on Hwy. 75 MM 201-202, restrooms

  Springs are at the edge of teh Salmon River with 170 degree water flowing in and mixing with the river water.

- White Cloud Rafting, 635 Edna McGown Ave, 800-751-raft, whitecloudrafting.com, one day river rafting, kayak trips, float trips, fishing

- White Otter Outdoor Adventures, Yankee Fork Rd, 208-788-5005, www.whiteotter.com, rafting, float trips, fishing, boat rentals

*Dining*

- Backcountry Bistro, 21 Ace of Diamonds St, 208-744-7000, backcountrybistro.com, 11:30-2:30 Tues-Sat, 6-9 on Fri-Sat, beer and wine

  Innovative Asian fusion cuisine and a prix fix seasonal menu in an upscale setting with white tablecloths and regional choices.

- *Bridge St Burger & Brew, Hwy. 75, 208-774-2208, bridgestgrill.com, indoor and outdoor dining, 3-close Thurs-Sat,

  Casual, good comfort food like ribs, burgers and salmon served with potato and corn on the cob. Also serves a nice Cobb salad. Outdoor seating is situated over the river for great views.

- *Elk Mountain Resort Restaurant (Pot Belly Cafe), 12655 Hwy. 21 4m W, 208-774-2202, elkmountainrv.com, breakfast, lunch and dinner, occasional live music

  Prime Rib, BBQ, house made soup, and homemade pie

- Mountain Village Express, 3 Eva Falls Ave, 208-774-3661, mountainvillage.com, breakfast, lunch and dinner

  Very casual setting, part of gas station.

- Papa Brunee's, 37 Ace of Diamonds, 208-774-2536, 208-774-2536, beer and wine, 4-9pm, indoor and outdoor seating

  Pasta, pizza and burgers.

- Peaks and Perks, Hwy. 21, 208-720-0078, coffee, ice cream, bagels

- Redfish Restaurant & Gazebo, Hwy. 75, 208-774-3536, serving breakfast, lunch and dinner, beer and wine, indoor and outdoor eating, reservations recommended in summer, under $25

  Emphasis on local and regional favorites with lake views in a rustic lodge atmosphere.

- Sawtooth Hotel, 755 Ace of Diamonds St, 208-721-2459, www.sawtoothhotel.com/stanley-dining/, indoor and outdoor dining

  Homemade traditional meals are served in the light dining room.

- Smiley Creek Lodge, 16546 N Hwy. 75, 208-774-3547, smileycreeklodge.com, open year round, 8am-9pm

  Full service restaurant with deli and ice cream parlor.

- *Stanley Baking Company and Cafe, 250 Wall St, 208-774-6573, www.stanleybakingco.com, indoor and outdoor dining, 7:30-2pm, under $10

  Lovely bakery with a wide selection of baked goods like cinnamon rolls, scones and cookies, breakfast entrees, lunch salads and sandwiches and Hailey Coffee Co. Vegetarian options.

- Stanley Sluice Alehouse, 16546 N Hwy. 75, 208-774-3547, smileycreeklodge.com/restaurant/, 8am-9pm (might be the same as smiley creek lodge restaurant above)

## Camping

- Chinook Bay Campground, 1.5m S on Hwy. 75 and 1m S on FR 214, 13 sites, drinking water, flush toilets, fee, ski trails, hiking, biking, fishing, boating

  Located on Redfish lake Creek near Little Redfish Lake with lots of pines and great views.

- Elk Creek Campground, Hwy 21 3m W of Stanley, vault toilets, drinking water, great bird and animal watching

- Elk Mountain RV Resort, 12655 Hwy. 21, 208-774-2202, full service restaurant, showers, full hook ups, laundry,

  Upper and lower campground. The lower is well shaded while the upper has better satellite access.

- Upper and Lower O'Brien Campground, Hwy. 75 15m W, 10 sites, picnic table, potable water, vault toilets, fishing

- Sawtooth National Recreation Area, 877-444-6777, reservations have to be made 4 days in advance and the 37 campgrounds fill up quickly, www.reserveusa.com

  The place is huge with over 750,000 acres, 700 miles of trails, 300 mountain lakes and 40 peaks rising over 10,000ft.

- Sheep Trail Campground, Hwy 21 W for 10m and FR 613, vault toilets, picnic area, trails

- Smiley Creek Lodge, 16546 Hwy. 75, 208-774-3547, smileycreeklodge.com, Yurts, showerhouse, laundry, wifi

  Some sites offer shaded privacy,

- Stanley Lake, paved Stanley Lake Rd W on Hwy. 21, 17 sites, vault toilets, drinking water, scenic overlook, trails

- Trap Creek Campground, Hwy 21, 12m W of Stanley, 6670ft elevation, vault toilets, hiking and biking trails

- Valley Creek Lodge & RV park, 1060 Eva Falls Ave, 208-774-3606, stanleyidaho.com, hook ups, no separate bathrooms

  A few RV spots are in the motel parking lot

## *Lodging*

- Beckwith's Lodge, off Hwy. 75, www.beckwithlodge.com, $325 nightly, hot tub, laundry

  Lodge was built on site by hand and has four bedrooms and 2 baths

- Bridge Street Cabins, brdigestgrill.com/Bridge_St_Cabins.html, 2 cabins,

  Cabins are comfortably rustic and basic with kitchens and located on the Salmon River. Amenities include flat screen tv and oil lamps.

- Danner's Log Cabin Motel, 1 Wall St, 208-774-3539, dannerslogcabins.com, 3 night minimum, 9 cabins, $80-140, dog friendly

  Lodgepole pine cabins are spread across a grassy lawn (pretty close together), no shade. Cabins are cozy and simple but modernized.

- Diamond D Ranch, 42m N of Stanley, 800-222-1269, www.diamonddranch-idaho.com, cabins and lodge rooms, swimming pool, hot tub, lake, fishing, hiking, swingset, horseback riding, archery, target shooting, $1270-1550 for adult for a week, all inclusive

  Rooms are modernized upscale rustic with lodgepole pine furnishings and wood floors.

- Idaho Rocky Mountain Ranch, 208-774-3544, idahorocky.com, 14 cabins and 3 lodge rooms, laundry, wifi in the lodge, hot springs pool, mountain bikes, fishing, all inclusive $187pp per day,

  All cabins have a fireplace

- Jerry's Country Store, Cabins & Motel, 55 Lower Stanley, 208-774-3566, lowerstanley.com/JerrysStore.asp, cabins and motel rooms, pet friendly, $90

  Located on the bank of the Salmon River in Lower Stanley with excellent views. Basic motel rooms have an updated kitchenette

- Meadow Creek Inn & Spa, 955 Eva Falls Ave, 208-774-3611, www.meadowcreekinn.com, 6 rooms, $99-109pp includes spa treatment, hot tub

  Rooms are individually themed decorated, each sleeps four

- Mountain Village Resort, 3 Eva Falls Ave, 208-774-3661, mountainvillage.com, 61 rooms, hot springs, pull thru RV spaces with hook ups, laundry, $90-140, pets welcome

  Basic motel rooms

- Redfish Lake Lodge, Hwy. 75, 208-774-3536, lodge rooms and cabins, wifi, $85-559, no pets, bike rentals, boating, fishing, day hikes from the lodge, horseback riding, swimming in the lake, visitor's center, laundry

  Rustic lodge has a lounge and general store. Cabins run the gamut from rustic to more luxurious with prices to match. Lodge rooms are basic. Reservations do fill up quickly, especially for the nicer cabins.

 Redfish Lake

Wikipedia, creative commons attribution, Karthikc123

- Redwood Stanley Cabins, 83 Hwy. 75, 208-774-3531, redwood-stanley.com, some with kitchen, wifi, $75-100

  Located on the river with great views of the mountains and a variety of outdoor seating options to enjoy the views. Simple cabins are carpeted with paneled walls.

- Riverside Motel & Sawtooth Rentals, 560 Mcgowan Ave, 208-774-3409, riversidemotel.biz, no pets, raft and kayak rental, $125-155

  7 lodge rooms front the river with decks for great views. Units also have kitchens and dishes. Rooms inside are simple motel rooms.

- Sawtooth Hotel, 755 Ace of Diamonds St, 208-721-2459, sawtoothhotel.com, shared and private baths, wifi, $70-100

  Located "downtown" such as it is, this log hotel is rustic with simple comforts. Rooms are located above the restaurant and do experience noise during restaurant hours.

- Smiley Creek Lodge, 16546 N Hwy. 75, 208-774-3547, smileycreeklodge.com, open year round, cabins, lodge rooms, teepees, $70-110

  Lodge rooms have private baths, cabins do not.

- Stanley High Country Inn, 21 Ace of Diamonds St, 208-774-7000, highcountryinn.biz , full American breakfast, no pets, hot tub

  Rooms are spacious with rustic furnishings and dark colors. Some rooms have kitchenettes. A sitting room and deck are available for guest use.

- Stanley Town Square Vacation Rentals, stanleytownsquare.com/vacation-rentals, 3 units with 2 bedrooms, laundry, $220 night

- Valley Creek Lodge, 1060 Eva Falls Ave, 208-774-3606, stanleyidaho.com, kitchens, fishing, no pets

  Basic motel rooms

## Clayton GPS:44.15N, 114.23W ; Elevation: 5489ft

### Getting Oriented
- Off Hwy. 75

### Practicalities
- Grocery/Laundromat

  Old Sawmill Station, 218 Hwy. 75, 208-838-2400, deli, convenient mart and laundromat

- Visitor Information

  www.claytonidaho.org

*Activities*

- Clayton Museum, 1 Ford St, 208-838-2467

- Custer Motorway, loop trail goes from Sunbeam E on Hwy. 75 to Hwy. 93 N to Challis then west on FR 070 to Custer and a S turn at Bonanza on Yankee Fork Rd.

  This historic motorway was once the route of Gold miners. Road climbs up to 8800 ft.

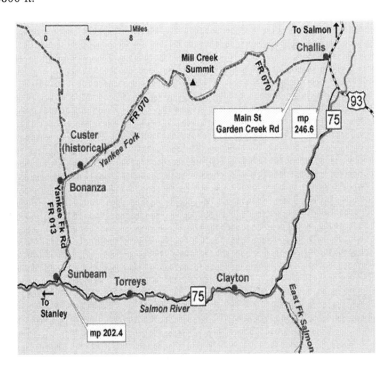

# Map of Custer and Clayton

(courtesy of fishandgame.idaho.gov)

*Dining*

- Hoodoo Saloon, 15 Silver St, 208-838-2252

*Camping*

- Bonanza CCC Reservation Campground, 11m E on hwy. 75 then N at Sunbeam 7m N on FR 13, 6200ft elevation, 12 sites for group camping, fishing, West Fork of the Yankee Fork Trailhead 1/2m N of campground

- Holman Creek Campground, 28m NE on Hwy. 75, 5600ft elevation, 10 sites, picnic tables, vault toilets, potable water, fishing

- Old Sawmill Station, 218 Hwy. 75, 208-838-2400, deli, convenient mart and laundromat, RV pull through, hook ups

- Torreys Resort & RV Park, Hwy. 75 MM 210, 888-838-2313, log cabins, RV park, laundry, showers, store, hook up

## Lodging

- May Family Ranch, 500 North Squaw Creek Rd, 3m W of Clayton, 208-838-2407, www.mayfamilyranch.com, bed and breakfast rooms, cabins and bunkhouse, floating, fishing, river running, hiking, cross-country skiing, RV hookups

  Bed and breakfast accommodations in the ranch house with simple rooms. Lounge are includes books for guest use and small kitchenette. A deck is also available.

- Torreys Resort & RV Park, Hwy. 75 MM 210, 888-838-2313, log cabins, RV park, laundry, showers, store, 8 cabins, picnic tables, $83-140

  Cabins are rustic and simple with basic modern conveniences and very dated decor.

# Challis GPS: 44.30N, 114.13W ; Elevation: 5253ft

## Getting Oriented

- Challis was platted in 1876 and while many of the small mining towns around have declined into ghost towns, Challis itself has thrived as the central economic center of the area. As such, it's a mixture of Historic Main Street and strip mall edges.

- Just N of the intersection of Hwy. 75 and 93, on Hwy. 93 58 m East of Stanley

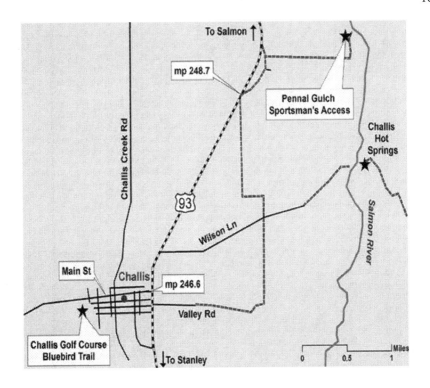

## Map of Challis
fishandgame.idaho.gov

### *Practicalities*

- Visitor Information

  Challis Messenger, a free visitor newspaper,
  www.challismessenger.com/specialPubs/CHMGuide2013.pdf

  Challis Ranger District, 208-879-4100, 8am-4:30

  Parks and Recreation Department, Hwy. 93/75 intersection, 208-879-5244

  challischamber.com

- Grocery

  Lambs Foodtown, 1307 Hwy. 93, 208-879-4456, subway inside,

- Library

  Challis Public Library, 6th and Main, 208-879-4267

*Parks*

- City Park, Hwy. 93, playgrounds, skate park

*Activities*

- *Land of the Yankee Fork State Park, Hwy. 93 and 75, elevation 5000ft, 208-879-5244, fee

  520 Acre park highlights, in multiple units (see Custer in Stanley), frontier and mining history in Idaho.

- Land of Yankee Fork Interpretive Center, Hwy 93 and Hwy. 75 intersection, 9am-5pm, fee, restrooms, gold panning, audiovisual programs

- Bayhorse Ghost Town, many mining remains are still on site,

  Interesting Charcoal Kilns are on site in addition to the ruins from the Mining town.

  Heads up: rattlesnake territory and lots of dangerous mine remains. Area is signed and fenced off to keep visitors away from the dangers.

- Bayhorse Recreation Site, 801 Blue Mtn Rd, 10m SW of Challis on Hwy. 75, 8600ft elevation, boating, camping, vault toilets, fishing, little shade

- Challis Bridge Recreation Site, 2m S on hwy. 93, boat ramp, vault toilets, picnic tables

- Challis Golf Course Bluebird Trail, Main St W 1.1m to Emily Ln S .2m to golf course parking area. 1m paved trail with bluebird boxes arranged on the trail.

- Challis Hot Springs, 5025 Hot Springs Rd, 4m S of Challis, 208-879-4442, www.challishotsprings.com, RV and tent camping, bed and breakfast, two soaking pools at 100 and 105 degrees, restrooms, showers

  The pools are continually circulated so they don't have much growth and limited need for chemical treatments.

- Cottonwood Recreation Site, 1151 Blue Mtn Rd, 14m N, 208-756-5400, vault toilets, dump station, potable water, fishing, camping, boating, picnic tables, fire rings,

- Horse Creek Outfitters, 208-879-5084, www.horsecrkoutfitters.com, archery, game hunting, fishing

- Mile High Outfitters, 127 Stephens Rd, 208-879-4500, www.milehighoutfitters.com, big game trips, fishing

- Morgan Creek Recreation Site, N on hwy. 93 and W on Morgan Creek Rd, 4 campsites, vault toilet, potable water, trail into the No Return Wilderness

- Salmon River Scenic Run Outfitters, 2010 Hot Springs Rd, 208-879-5394, www.scenicriver.com, relaxing river trips, fishing

- White Cloud Outfitters, 1500 Upper Hot Springs Rd, 208-879-4574, www.whitecloudoutfitters.com

- Wilderness Outfitters, 208-473-4448, www.idahowilderness.com, fishing, horseback riding, hunting, backpacking support

*Dining*

- Antonio's Pizza and Pasta, 431 Main, 208-879-2210, challisidaho.com/splash.html?link_id8104, 11am-9pm, beer and wine, inside and outside dining

  Salad bar, pizza, pasta and entrees like Veal Parmesan. Sandwiches are also available. Dough is hand tossed.

- Challis Lanes & Drive In, 511 Hwy. 93N, 208-879-4452

- Challis Lodge & Lounge, 1220 Main St, 208-879-2251 , beer and wine, 4pm-12am

  Fresh prepared food, burgers, fries, soups and sandwiches.

- Challis Village Inn Restaurant, 300 & 310 Hwy. 93, 208-879-2239, challisvillageinn.com, wifi

  Steak, seafood, chicken and sandwiches. Mexican menu available on week days. Ice cream.  Non descript dining room with a chain like aura.

- *Nummyz, 11 m N of Challis on Hwy. 93 MM 257, 208-879-2047, 10:30-8, closed Mon-Tues, wifi, beer , under $10

  Road side, open air cafe with enclosed patio serving simple but unique fare including Korean BBQ.

- Pioneer Motel & RV Park, Hwy. 93, 208-879-6791, www.challismotelrvpark.com, coffee shop

- Tea Cup Cafe & Bakery, 200 E Main, 208-879-5050, facebook page updated regularly, 7am-8pm, espresso bar

  Situated in a home, the cafe and bakery serves breakfast and lunch including soups and sandwiches.

- Y-Inn Cafe, 1200 N Main St, 208-879-4426, yinncafe.com, 7am-7pm,

  Typical diner with homemade pies, biscuits and gravy and chicken fried steak. Lounge area for tv watching with comfy seats. Pizza delivery from 5-8pm.

*Camping*

- Bayhorse Lake Campground, Hwy 75W for 5.5m to Old Road, right for 2.8m onto Bayhorse Creek Rd 8.5m, elevation 8500 ft (steep drive to site), 9 sites, vault toilets, picnic area, boating, fishing,

- Blue Mountain Fish Pond Camping Area, Main St to 2nd St, turn left until it dead ends

- Challis Hot Springs, 5025 Hot Springs Rd, 4m S of Challis, 208-879-4442, www.challishotsprings.com, RV and tent camping, bed and breakfast, two soaking pools

  Campground is on the Salmon River.

- Challis Valley RV Resort , 211 Ramshorn Ln, 208-879-2393, challisvalleyrvresort.com, 70 sites,  large pull thrus, full hook ups, wifi, showers, dump, laundry

  This is a very large campground with some open and shaded spaces, all with mountain vistas.

- Pioneer Motel & RV Park, Hwy. 93, 208-879-6791, www.challismotelrvpark.com, 40 sites, pull through, showers

*Lodging*

- Challis Lodge, 1220 Main St, 208-879-2251

- Challis Hot Springs, 5025 Hot Springs Rd, 208-879-4442, www.challishotsprings.com, bed and breakfast, $95, 7 rooms and suites

  Resort has two soaking pools. Rooms are uniquely decorated

- Creek Side Inn, 630 E North Ave, 208-879-5608, www.creeksideinnbandb.com, wifi, variety of accommodations

  Renovated Victorian home with attractive furnishings

- Northgate Inn , 1110 Hwy. 93N, 208-879-2490, challismotel.com,  $40-70, wifi

  Basic motel rooms

- Pioneer Motel & RV Park, Hwy. 93, 208-879-6791,
  www.challismotelrvpark.com, bed and breakfast, cabins, motel rooms, campfire
  ring, playground, picnic tables, wifi,

  Rooms in the motel are simple and comfortable with some kitchenettes.

- Watermark Inn, 810 E North Ave, 208-879-5084, thewatermarkinn.com, dinner
  available, $90-125 includes breakfast

  Rooms are simply and attractively furnished with one two room option.

- The Challis Village Inn Motel and Restaurant, 310 Hwy. 93, 208-879-2239,
  challisvillageinn.com, variety of room options, wifi, air con, pet friendly

  Dated, dark decor typical motel room.

- Yankee Fork Retreat, 155 Dredge Camp Rd, 208-879-6791,
  www.yankeeforkretreat.com, 2 bedroom/2bath unit and bunk house

## Idaho County

- Idaho County is the largest county in Idaho, situated in North Central Idaho.
  Despite its size, however, there are not many populated areas. Grangeville is the
  largest town and the county seat. The Nez Perce reservation takes up a large
  part of the county.

**Elk City** GPS: 45.49N, 115.26W ; Elevation: 4006 ft

*Getting Oriented*
- Off Hwy. 14, E of Grangeville in the heart of the Nez Perce National Forest

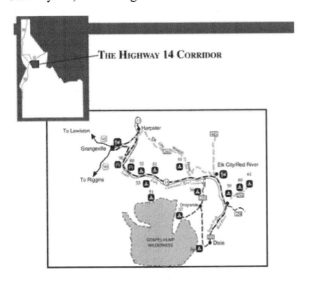

THE HIGHWAY 14 CORRIDOR

## Map of Hwy. 14

(courtesy of fs.usda.gov)

*Practicalities*

- Visitor Information

  Red River Ranger District/Elk City Ranger Station, 300 American River Rd, 208-842-2245, 7:30-4pm Mon-Fri

- Laundry

  Laundromat, Main St at Sinclair

*Activities*

- 14 Mile Trailhead, turn off Hwy. 14 on Red River Rd for 24 miles of paved and gravel, access to two trails, 501, 580 into the Frank Church River of No Return Wilderness, vault toilets, interpretive signs

- Historic Red River Ranger Station, turn off Hwy 14 on Red River Rd 10 miles, restrooms, RV dumping, potable water, interpretive signs

- Red River Wildlife Management Area, mp 46.7 Hwy. 14 turn onto FR 222 10m, great bird watching.

- Magruder Corridor (FR 468), from Red River Rd and Hwy. 14 to Darby Mt, 181m

  The one lane mostly unimproved road traverses an undeveloped forest corridor with beautiful views of the Bitterroot and Clearwater Mountains. The first ten miles are paved, but very windy, and take travelers to the Old Ranger Station.

*Media Connection: for a trail guide for this route, go to http://www.everytrail.com/guide/magruder-corridor-guide*

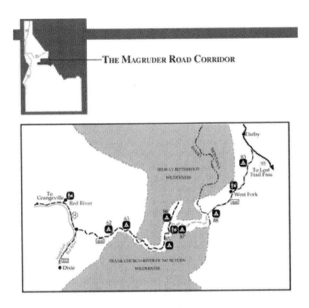

THE MAGRUDER ROAD CORRIDOR

## Map of River of No Return Wilderness
(courtesy of fs.usda.gov)

### *Eating*
- Elk City Saloon & Cafe, 208-842-2311, facebook page
- Elk Creek Station and Cafe, 110 Main St, 208-842-2551, facebook page, 7am-7pm

### *Camping*
- Red River Campground, Hwy. 14 W 2.8m to Red River Rd East 19.6m, 40 sites, picnic table, fire ring, vault toilet, fishing, hiking
- Sleepy Hollow RV Park, 150 Ridgeway Dr #17, 208-842-2268, 14 sites, potable water, fire rings, full hookup, pull thru, hiking, gold panning

### *Lodging*
- Elk City Hotel/Motel, 289 Main St, 208-842-5336, www.elkcityhotelidaho.com, currently for sale, wifi,

## Dixie GPS: 45.33N, 115.27 W ; Elevation: 5620 feet

### *Getting Oriented*
- Dixie is in the middle of nowhere, literally, on FR 222

*Activities*
- Silver Spur Outfitters & Lodge, Inc, 2742 Dixie Rd, 208-842-2417, silverspurlodge.com, hunting, backcountry trips, fishing

**Lowell** GPS: 46.08N, 115.35 W ;  Elevation: 1486 feet

*Getting Oriented*
- Off Hwy. 12, near the Montana border. Here the Lochsa and Selway river come together to make up the middle fork of the Clearwater River.

## Map of Hwy. 12 and Clearwater National Forest
(From wikimedia GNU Free Documentation License, Creative commons)

*Visitor Information*
- Lowell Kiosk, at the Hwy. 12 and Selway Rd intersection

- Moose Creek Ranger District/Fenn Ranger Station, 831 Selway Rd, 5m S of Hwy. 12, 208-926-4258, 7:30-4pm Mon-Fri, fishing pond, picnic area

This 1930 ranger station is on the National Register of Historic Places. Walk the self-guided walking tour through the landscaped grounds. Visitor information is available inside.

*Media Connection: The Forest Service has made a brochure for the Moose Creek District. Access it here, http://www.fs.usda.gov/Internet/FSE_DOCUMENTS/fsm91_055704.pdf*

- O'Hara Kiosk, at O'Hara Bar Bridge on Selway Rd.

## *Activities*

- Canyon Creek Trail 107, 7.4m past Lowell on Hwy. 12, across from Apgar Campground

  Narrow canyon trail

- Fenn Pond, 5m up Selway River Rd, stocked pond and boardwalk nature trail, fishing is catch and release

- Lochsa River Outfitters, 9133 Hwy. 12, www.lochsariveroutfitters.com, 208-926-4149, hunting trips

- O'Hara Creek Trail (#713), 4m up the Selway River Scenic dr, 2490ft elevation, 2.1m out and back trail is winding and crosses the creek several times. In high water, this can be dangerous.

- Rackliff Ridge Trail, #702, 9m on Selway River Rd, 6m trail climbs 5000 ft with great views

- Selway River Scenic Drive (FR 223), paved to O'Hara Creek Bridge then dirt/gravel.

  Road travels through the Selway-bitterroot Wilderness with access to campgrounds and hiking trails.

- Three Rivers Resort and Rafting, Hwy. 12, 208-926-4430, www.threeriversrafting.com, float trips and mild rafting, fishing, kayaks

## *Dining*

- Three Rivers Resort and Rafting, Hwy. 12, 208-926-4430, www.threeriversrafting.com, full bar, flat screen tvs

  Full menu with burgers, steaks, fish and salads.

- Wilderness Inn Motel, 8883 Hwy. 12, 208-926-4706, wildinn2.com

Large menu serves sandwiches, fast food, burgers and homemade pies, ice cream and milkshakes

## Camping

- Apgar Campground, 7.4m E on Hwy. 12, 1520ft elevation, 7 sites, fee, vault toilet, fishing, rafting, kayaking, swmming, trail south of campground

- CCC Campground, on Selway Rd FR 223, 1550 ft elevation, 3 sites, toilet, fishing, hiking trail #734

  The campground sits along the Selway River and near the Fenn Pond.

- Johnson Bar Campground, on Selway Rd 4m, 7 sites, picnic, drinking water, toilet, swimming in the river, rafting, fishing, mountain biking, hiking fee

- O'Hara Bar Campground, 7m on Selway Rd, 32 sites, picnic, toilet, potable water, fishing, fee

  Very nice views of the river from this large campground.

- Rackliff Campground, on Selway Rd 9m, 6 sites, picnic area, vault toilet, fishing, fee, access to Rackliff Ridge Trail

## Lodging

- Three Rivers Resort and Rafting, Hwy. 12, 208-926-4430, www.threeriversrafting.com, cabins and motels, air con, campfire ring, wifi, heated pool , hot tubs, $59-165

- Ryan's Wilderness Inn Motel, 8883 Hwy. 12, 208-926-4706, wildinn2.com, $57-67, air con

  Basic motel rooms, and all have had smokers as resident.

# Syringa GPS: 41.31N, 120.10 W ; Elevation: 4652 feet

## Getting Oriented

- MM 90 on Hwy. 12

## Activities

- Lower Selway River Trail (Forest Trail #4), 50m with 4200 ft elevation gain out and back

  Trail follows the Selway River with a few river crossings

  Heads up: rattlesnake and bear territory and really hot in the summer

### Dining

- Syringa Cafe, 7743 Hwy. 12 (see River Dance Lodge below), seasonal, $25pp prix fix for dinner, lunch 11-5pm Sat and Sun

  Dinner is served in one seating starting at 7pm

### Lodging

- River Dance Lodge, 7743 Hwy. 12, 208-926-4300, 800-451-6034, riverdancelodge.com, wifi, fishing, biking, all inclusive rafting/hiking resort, 2-3 bedrooms, $109-359

  Rustic elegance in the individual cabins with small kitchenettes and lofts. Provides a full service adventure experience as well (but guests are welcome to just relax).

## Kooskia GPS: 46.139N, 115.97 W ; Elevation: 1293 feet

### Getting Oriented

- Located at a bend in the Clearwater River, Kooskia is at Hwy. 12 and Hwy 13

  *Media Connection: NPNHT Auto Tour Wallow Or to Kooskia ID pdf*
  *http://www.fs.usda.gov/Internet/FSE_DOCUMENTS/stelprdb5410770.pdf*

### Practicalities

- Visitor Information

  Kooskia Crossing Welcome Center, Hwy. 12 and Hwy. 13, outdoor exhibit

  www.kooskia.com

  Lochsa/Powell Ranger District, 502 Lowry St, 208-926-4274, 7:30-4:30 Mon-Fri.

- Laundry

  Kooskia Western Motor Inn, 6 South Main St, 208-926-0166, laundromat on site

- Library

  Kooskia Library, 26 S Main, 208-926-4539

### Shopping

- Eldon's Sausage and Jerky Supply, 22 Main St, 800-352-9453, www.eldonsausage.com

*Activities*

- Kooskia National Fish Hatchery, 3m E of Kooskia, 208-926-4272, 7:30am-4pm

- Kohls Outfitting, 208-926-4338, www.kohlsoutfitting.com, fully and semi-guided hunting, fishing

- Kooskia Crossing, at Hwy. 12 and Hwy. 13 intersection,

  Interpretive signs and metal sculpture

- Kooskia Internment Camp, Hwy 12 30m NE from Kooskia, www.uidaho.edu/class/kicap/about

  Undergoing archaeological research but open for summer field institutes.

  *Learn More About it: 120,000 individuals with Japanese heritage were forcibly relocated in 1942, 256 males were located in this internment camp. The men worked on Hwy. 12. Almost nothing remains of this remote camp but minimal excavation is being conducted.*

- Lewis and Clark National Historical Trail

  This part of the trail was one of the most difficult portions that Lewis and Clark faced

- Chief Looking Glass Camp, East exit off Hwy. 12 at MP 75 and cross the bridge. Take a left to the Kooskia National Fish Hatchery and travel 2m to a fork in the road to the interpretive sign.

  The camp is named after Chief Looking Glass who was attacked by Captain Stephen Whipple in 1863 and many of the villagers were killed. Looking Glass up until the attack a neutral observer, joined the rest of the Nez Perce bands fleeing the soldiers.

  *Learn More About it: The National park service has put together a brochure that explains the Nez Perce War in 1877. It can be downloaded here, http://www.nps.gov/history/history/online_books/biho/greene/index.htm*

*Dining*

- China Cafe, 118 South Main St, 208-926-4800

- Coffee & Cream, 114 North Main St, 208-926-7140

- Kooskia Cafe, 6 N Main St, 208-926-4351, wifi, for sale

- Silver Dollar, 6 S. Main St, 208-926-8860, Burgers, fries

- Rivers Cafe, 18 N Main, 208-926-0986

Burgers, fries, tater tots

*Camping*
- River Junction RV Park, Hwy. 12, 208-926-7865, 50 sites, hookup, pull thru

*Lodging*
- Kooskia Western Motor Inn, 6 South Main St, 208-926-0166, westernmotorinn.com, 20 units, laundry, wifi, playground

  Basic motel

- Reflections Inn, 6873 Hwy. 12, 208-926-0855, www.reflectionsinn.com, 8 rooms sleep 2-4, hot tub, wifi, breakfast included, all private baths, laundry, $108-146

  Porch welcomes visitor to enjoy the outdoors and a sitting area is also available inside.

- Southfork River Ranch, 3341 Hwy. 13, 208-926-4514, 208-507-1514, southforkriverranch.com, 2 cabins, pol, hot tub, fishing, archery, picnics, all inclusive, $225 pp per night

# Stites GPS: 46.5N, 115.58W ; Elevation: 1306 ft

*Getting Oriented*
- South of Kooskia on Hwy. 13

*Practicalities*
- Grocery

  Stites Grocery, 215 Main St, 208-926-7300

*Dining*
- Southfork Cafe, 202 Main St, 208-926-8816

  American favorites like chicken fried steak, burgers, soup and sandwiches.

*Lodging*
- Idaho Sportsman Lodge, 103 East St, 208-926-4766, www.idahosportsmanlodge.com, 4 large units that sleep 8, $89-200 depending on number of rooms used

  Lodgepole pine dominates these cabins with full amenities and kitchens,

# Kamiah GPS: 46.13N, 116.1W ; Elevation: 1240 ft

*Getting Oriented*
- Kamiah is to the west of the Clearwater River and to the South of Hwy 12

*Practicalities*
- Visitor Information

  Kamiah Chamber of Commerce, 518 Main St, 208-935-2290, www.kamiahcahmber.com, wifi, interpretive signs

  Kamiah Ranger Station, 903 3rd St, 208-935-2513

- Grocery

  Cloninger's Harvest Foods, 508 3rd St, 208-935-2151, full service grocery

- Restrooms

  Castle Valley Library, 2 Castle Valley Drive, 435-259-9998, limited hours

*Activities*
- Murals, scattered around parks and buildings are a variety of paintings and metal works as outdoor art

- First Indian Presbyterian Church, 518 Main St,

  Church was constructed in 1873 and is still in use today. It is the oldest Protestant church in the United States

- Five Mile Interpretive Site, MM 54.5 Hwy. 12

- Heart of the Monster, MP 68.5 Hwy. 12, 208-843-7001,

  An audio station speaks the monster and coyote creation legend of the Nimipuu. Here, Coyote defeated a monster and created the people.

- It Se-Ye-Ye-Casino, 419 3rd St, 208-935-7860, www.crcasino.com

- Kamiah Historical Society Museum, 518 Main St, 10-4 Tues-Fri, seasonal

- Asa Smith Mission and Lewis and Clark Long Camp Historical Site, MM 68 Hwy. 12, 1m E of Kamiah, 208-935-0764, interpretive signs

  Here, Lewis and Clark spent 3 weeks among the Nez Perce in 1806 waiting for snow melt so they could continue homeward.

- Weitas Creek Outfitters, 211 Winona Rd, www.idahooutfitter.com, 208-983-9267, hunting, fishing, trail rides

- Parks

  Riverfront Park, Hwy. 12, play areas, picnic shelter, nature trail runs along the river

## Dining

- Hearthstone Bakery and tea House, 502 Main St, 208-935-2322, www.hearthstonebakery.com/, 6am-3pm, breakfast, pastries, lunch, artisan bread

- The Hub Bar & Grill, 406 Main St, 208-935-2211, facebook page, 6:30-2:30am, mostly under $10

  Local favorite bar and restaurant serving steak, burgers and broasted chicken. Also lots of fried apps, pie and salad.

- Kamiah Pizza Factory, 814 3rd St, 208-935-2134, kamiah.pizzafactory.com, 11am-10pm, under $20

- Pizza, salad, sandwiches, soup and pasta.

- Moose River Grill, 501 4th, 208-935-2821

- Rivers Cafe, 18 N Main St, 208-926-0986

  Burgers and fries in classic cafe

- Sacajawea Cafe, 4243 Hwy. 12, 208-935-2556, www.lewisclarkresort.com/cafe.htm, 7am-8pm, until 3pm on Sun, closed Mon.

  Homemade soups and daily specials.

## Camping

- Lewis Clark Resort, 4243 Hwy. 12, 208-935-2556, www.lewisclarkresort.com, 165 RV sites, pool, jacuzzi, laundry, full hook ups

- Long Camp RV Park, 4192 Hwy. 12, 208-935-7922, www.longcamprvpark.com, 22 sites, hookup, 40 tent sites, wifi, showers, laundry,

  Some sites are riverfront. Shady spots abut the river bank.

## Lodging

- Clearwater 12 Motel, 108 E 3rd St, 208-935-2671, www.clearwater12motel.net, 29 rooms, casino

Basic motel rooms

- Flying B Ranch, 2900 Lawyer Creek Rd, 208-935-0755, www.flyingbhunting.com, 19 rooms, $1200-6500, wifi, shooting, fishing, hunting

- Hearthstone Lodge, 3250 Hwy. 12, 877-563-4348, hearthstone-lodge.com, 5 rooms, $125-235

  Old fashioned, elaborate decor in a large lodge overlooking the Clearwater River.

- Kamiah Inn Motel, 216 3rd St, 208-935-0040, kamiahinn.com, wifi, some kitchens, some suites, $49-75

  Basic motel rooms

- Lewis Clark Resort, 4243 Hwy. 12, 208-935-2556, www.lewisclarkresort.com, 21 rooms, 7 cabins, pool, hot tub, laundry, petting zoo area

  Rooms and cabins are basic with kitchenettes and simple furnishings.

- Quilt House Bed & Breakfast Inn, 247 Flying Elk Dr, 208-935-7668, www.quilthousebedandbreakfast.com, shared baths, $125-165 with full breakfast, quilt classes offered

  Made of lodge pole pine and decorated with quilts and country decor, the home has a reading lounge and a deck for guest use.

- Sundown Motel, 1004 3rd St, 208-935-2568

## Harpster GPS: 45.59N, 115.57W ; Elevation: 1575 ft.

### Getting Oriented
- 10m E of Grangeville on Hwy. 13

### Activities
- Elk City Wagon Rd, go into Harpster and turn at the sign describing the road, 53 miles to Elk City, single lane road, unpaved, open to ATV, motorbikes, UTV, 4-wheel drive

*Media Connection: The Forest Service has created a very detailed brochure for this route, http://stayontrails.com/assets/content/docs/Elk-City-wagon-road-brochure.pdf*

*Camping*
- Harpster Riverside RV Park, 2895 Hwy 13, 208-983-2312, 30 sites, 6 Yurts, water, dump, full hookups, laundry, fishing, rafting

# Grangeville GPS: 45.55N, 116.7 W ; Elevation: 3399 feet

*Getting Oriented*
- To the East of Hwy. 95. Hwy. 13 starts at 95 and heads E.

*Practicalities*
- Visitor Information

  Grangeville Idaho Visitor Center, Hwy 95 at Pine, Grangevilleidaho.com, 9-5 in summer, 10-2 Mon, Weds, Fri in Winter, handcrafted art displays, restrooms

  Nez Perce-Clearwater National Forest, 104 Airport Rd, 208-983-1950, 7:30-4:30 Mon-Fri.

- Grocery

  The Health Food Store, 221 West Main St, 208-983-1276

  Askers Harvest Foods, 415 West Main, 208-983-0680

*Activities*
- Bicentennial Historical Museum, 305 North College, 208-983, 2573, 1-5 Weds-Fri, seasonal

  Collection of Nez Perce artifacts, mining exhibit and pioneer displays

- Camas Prairie Byway, Grangeville on Hwy. 95 to Winchester

  Rolling landscape of oat, wheat and canola. In late May, you might see the fields filled with Camas blooms.

- Eimers Park, Hwy. 95 at Pine, 208-983-0460, visitor center is located here

  Mammoth replica can be seen at this park.

- Fish Creek Meadows, 7m S of Grangeville on Grangeville Salmon Rd, cross country skiing

- Fish Creek Meadows Loop, 3, 5 and 7m hiking/biking loop and snowshoe loop

  Rolling terrain trail starts at the Pavilion in the Fish Creek Campgrounds. Trail has some nice shade.

*Media Connection: Forest service has a kind of rough brochure of the trails and park, http://www.fs.usda.gov/Internet/FSE_DOCUMENTS/fsm91_055710.pdf*

- Mackay Bar Outfitters & Guest Ranch, 208-965-8355, mackaybarranch.com, guided hunts, fishing, hiking, cabins and rooms

- Pioneer Park, East end of Main St, playground, picnic areas, city pool

- Snowhaven Ski and Tubing Hill, Salmon Rd, 208-983-3866

## Eating

- Hilltop Restaurant, 500 East Main, 208-983-1714

  Very busy local restaurant especially at breakfast. Portions are large and food is American with specialities like home fries, biscuits and gravy and Belgium Waffles.

- One for the Road, 700 1/2 Main St, in the Gateway Inn parking lot, coffee drive thru

- Oscar's Restaurant, 101 E Main, 208-983-2106

  Standard diner fare with a dose of serious taxidermy.

- Palenque, 711 W Main St., 208-983-1335, 11am-8pm, Mexican

- Pizza Factory, 126 W Main St, 208-983-5555, grangeville.pizzafactory.com, chain

- Seasons Restaurant, 124 West Main, 208-983-4203, wine and beer

  Sandwiches, salads for lighter appetites and steaks, chicken, ribs and fish for those who are more hungry.

- The Gallery, 107 West North St, 208-983-2595, www.thegallerygrangeville.com, 10-5:30, closed Sun-Mon, beer and wine

  Art, gifts and lunch

- Twisted Cellar, 123 West Main St, 208-983-1580, facebook page updated regularly, 11am-8pm

  Serves a bit more interesting menu then most places in town including Tacos, Peanut Butter cake, and changing menu items.

## Camping

- Bear Den RV Resort, 16967 Hwy. 95 S, 800-530-2658, www.beardenrv.com, cabins, hookup, wifi, laundry, showers

Sites are mostly open, situated in a large meadow area.

- Fish Creek Campground, 7m S of Grangeville on Grangeville Salmon Rd,

- Hammer Creek Recreation Site, take Old hwy 95W to Canfield, 12 sites, drinking water, vault and flush toilets, dump station, fee

- Harpster Riverside RV Park, Hwy. 13, Harpster, 208-983-2312, harpsterriversidervpark.com, dumping, laundry, hookup

- Mountain View M/H RV Park, 127 Cunningham St, 800-983-2328, www.mountainviewmhrvpark.com, hookup, laundry, pull thru

- Sundown RV Park, 102 North C St, 208-983-9113, grangevillervpark.com, wifi, showers, hookups, picnic tables, laundry

### Lodging

- Downtowner Inn, 113 E North, 208-983-1110, www.grangevillemotel.com, wifi

Basic motel rooms

- Elkhorn Lodge, 822 W South 1st, 208-983-1500, elkhornlodge.wordpress.com, wifi

Typical motel rooms

- Evergreen Suites, 605 E Main, 888-832-5251, www.grangevillebnb.com, 3 rooms, two bedroom suites, kitchens, wifi, $75-95

Lively and colorful decor in simple surroundings

- Gateway Inn, 700 W Main St, 877-983-1463, www.idahogatewayinn.com, 28 units, wifi, pool, kitchenettes, suites, pool, breakfast included

Remodeled motel rooms

- Whitebird Summit Lodge, 2141 Old White Bird Hill Rd, 866-562-5398, www.whitebirdsummitlodge.com, $120 including full breakfast, private baths, wifi

Rooms have thematic decor and sleep 2-4.

**Cottonwood** GPS: 46.38N, 116.21 W ; Elevation: 3497 ft

## Getting Oriented

- Just to the West of Hwy. 95, Bus 95 runs through downtown. Cottonwood is N of Grangeville in the central pan-handle.

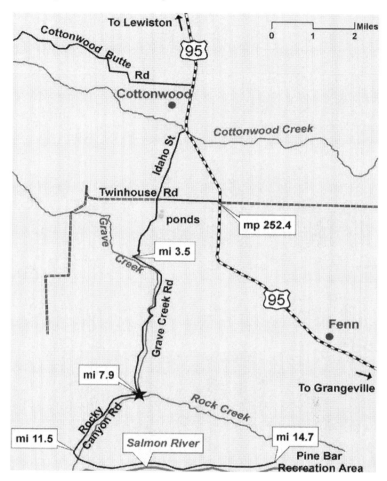

# Map of Fenn and Hwy. 95

(courtesy of fishandgame.idaho.gov)

- The area is central to the Nez Perce Historic Trail and the Lewis and Clark Historic Trail as well as access to both the Salmon and Clearwater Rivers

- North Idaho Correctional Institution, a minimum security facility is located here

## Practicalities

- Visitor Information

www.cottonwoodidaho.org

Cottonwood Field Office, 1 Butte Dr, 208-962-3245

- Grocery

  Cottonwood Foods, 305 Main St, 208-962-3631

  Riener's Grocery, 404 King St, 208-962-3811, 7:30-6:30

- Library

  Prairie Community Library, 506 King St, 208-962-3714

## Shopping

- Dog Bark Park & Dog Bark park Inn, Hwy. 95 at the Dog, 208-962-3647, www.dogbarkparkinn.com, 11-4pm, gift shop with major dog stuff, visitor center, art

## Events

- Raspberry Festival, held at the St Gertrude Monastery, August,

## Activities

- *Historical Museum at St Gertrude, 465 Keuterville Rd, 208-962-2059, www.historicalmuseumatstgertrude.org, 9:30-4:30, closed Sun-Mon, fee

  Museum started in 1931 in a still active Monastery. Exhibits focus on the history of the Benedictine Sisters, the Nez Perce and a selection of art.

- Cottonwood Butte Ski Area, 5m from Cottonwood, take Cottonwood Butte Rd to Radar Rd, 208-962-3624, 10-4pm Sat-Sun and 6-10pm Fri, ski and snowboard rental and lessons, warm meals

- Cottonwood Centennial Garden, Main St

- Cottonwood Farm Museum, fairgrounds

- Ferdinand park, 8m from Cottonwood

- Lawyers Canyon, off Hwy. 95, large trestle bridge crosses the canyon, interpretive sign

- Pine Bar Recreation Site, 11m S of Cottonwood on Graves Creek Rd, drinking water, boat ramp, vault toilets, fee, fishing

  Pine bar lies along the Lower Salmon River and is a frequent put-in spot for rafting

- Weis Rock Shelter, SW of Cottonwood off Hwy. 95 to Idaho St South to Grave Creek Rd 8m, in Grave's Creek Canyon

  This shelter was used by ancient peoples around 6000 BCE and was inhabited until about 600 years ago. The site was excavated in the 1960's. It was named after the amateur archeologists who excavated the site.

*Dining*
- Country Haus Restaurant & Village Motel, 407 Foster Ave, 208-962-3391, $35-50

  Full service American restaurant

- Jitterz Java & Deli, 415 Main St, 208-962-5222, 6:30-5:30

*Camping*
- Pine Bar Recreation Site, 11m S of Cottonwood, 6 sites, fire rings, picnic tables, drinking water, vault toilets, fee

*Lodging*
- Country Haus Restaurant & Village Motel, 407 Foster Ave, 208-962-3391, $35-50

- Dog Bark Park Inn, 2421 Hwy. 95, 208-962-3647, www.dogbarkparkinn.com, $86-116, continental breakfast, air con, pets are welcome

  Hard to miss this inn built in the shape of the dog. Chainsaw art works decorate the lawn and are for sale at the inn. Dog decor dominates

- *Inn at St. Gertrude, 465 Keuterville Rd, 208-451-4321, www.innatstgertrude.com, simple breakfast, wifi, $89-119

  Run by Sisters from the St Gertrude Monastery, the inn embodies the Benedictine values of healing hospitality, grateful simplicity and creative peacemaking. This includes a silent breakfast during the weekdays. Decor is warm and inviting and not at all sparse.

# Keuterville GPS: 46.2N, 116.26W ; Elevation: 4163ft

*Getting Oriented*
- West of Cottonwood on Keuterville Rd.

*Dining*
- Keuterville Pub & Grub, 1044 Keuterville Rd, 208-962-3090

# Greencreek GPS: 46.06N, 116.15W ; Elevation: 3189ft

### Getting Oriented
- Off hwy. 95 East on Jentges Rd

## Ferdinand GPS: 46.9N, 116.23W ; Elevation: 3720ft

### Getting Oriented
- Off Hwy. 95 to the West

## White Bird GPS: ; Elevation: 1560ft

### Getting Oriented
- Off Hwy. 95, East

### Practicalities
- Visitor Information

  visitwhitebird.com

  Salmon River Ranger District/Slate Creek Ranger Station, 304 Slate Creek Rd, 208-839-2211, 7:30-4pm Mon-Fri

- Laundry

  Swiftwater RV Park, 3154 Salmon River Ct, 208-839-2700, www.swiftwaterrv.com, laundromat

- Library

  White Bird Community Library, 245 River St, 208-839-2805, wifi 24/7

### Events
- White Bird Days and Rodeo, June, whitebirdrodeo.com

### Shopping
- Canyon House, 128 White Bird Rd, Hwy. 95, 208-839-2777, www.canyon-housewhitebird.com, light groceries, gifts, wine and beer

### Activities
- All Rivers Shuttle, 120 South Main, 800-785-7198, shuttles and guide, boat rentals

- Hells Canyon Jet Boat Trips and Lodging, 3252 Waterfront Dr, 208-839-2255, killgoreadventures.com, jet boat tours, fishing charters, jet boat shuttles

  70 mile round trip Hells Canyon tours are offered departing from White Bird.

- Skookumchuck Recreation Area, 1 Butte Dr, 5m S of Whitebird, 208-962-3245, picnic tables, vault toilets, swimming beach

- Slate Creek Recreation Site, 10m S of Whitebird on Hwy. 95, boat launch, vault toilets, dump station, fee

- Snake River National Recreation Trail (102), S on Hwy. 95 to Old Hwy. 95 at MM 222 (sign to Pittsburg Landing and Hammer Creek Recreation Area) go about 1m over a bridge and turn on Deer Creek Rd (FR 493) for 16.5m to FR 493A and turn left 1.3m to parking area

  Heads up: Both Deer Creek Rd and FR 493 are steep and winding paved gravel

- White Bird Battlefield, 2m N of Whitebird on old Hwy, 95, 208-843-7001

  Here, the first battle of the Nez Perce War was fought in 1877. The battlefield is named after a Nez Perce Chief White Bird

## Dining

- Canyon House, 128 White Bird Rd, Hwy. 95, 208-839-2777, www.canyon-housewhitebird.com , coffee and freeze drinks

- Mac's Supper Club, 140 River Rd, 208-839-2600, macssupperclub.com, 11-8pm, steak and seafood, under $20

  Serves a bit of everything from burgers and steak to prime rib to homemade lasagne.

- Silver Dollar Bar, 100 Main St, 208-839-2293, hearty breakfasts

## Lodging

- Canyon House, 128 White Bird Rd, Hwy. 95, 208-839-2777, www.canyon-house.com, 2 room suite with kitchen, $75

- Hells Canyon Jet Boat Trips and Lodging, 3252 Waterfront Dr, 208-839-2255, killgoreadventures.com, motel rooms, $65-75

- Kilgore Cabins/RV, 208-839-2255

- River Ranch Inn, 210 Robinson Ln, 208-839-2340

- White Bird Motel, 115 Bridge St, www.whitebirdmotel.com

## Camping

- Angel's Nook RV Park, 1m E of Hwy. 95, 208-839-2880, www.angelsnook.com, wifi

- Slate Creek Recreation Site, 10m S of Whitebird on Hwy. 95, 5 sites, fire rings, drinking water, vault toilets, dump station, boat ramp, fee

- Swiftwater RV Park, 3154 Salmon River Ct, 208-839-2700, www.swiftwaterrv.com, dumping, wifi, laundromat, restrooms, showers

# Warren GPS: 45.26N, 115.67W ; Elevation: 5906 ft

## Getting Oriented

- Off dirt Hwy. 21, E of Hwy. 95

- Closest thing to an old mining town you'll find in Idaho, partly a ghost town though at its peak, 5000 miners lived here.

   *Media Connection: You can pick up a Warren Walking Tour brochure in McCall at the Forest Ranger Station or check at the Warren Guard Station.*

Wikipedia Commons in the public domain, Faustus37

## Practicalities

- Warren Guard Station, Hwy 21 Warren Wagon Rd, information and exhibits in a 1926 building

*Activities*
- Twenty Mile Trail, on Warren Wagon Rd at the N end of Upper Payette Lake, 18m from McCall, 5600ft elevation, trail information board, 3m easy hike and then 3m more steep, bike or hike

- Victor Creek Trail, on Warren Wagon Rd past the Twenty Mile Trail, 21m from McCall, 12.5m long trail but do the first mile for views across meadows to the mountains

## Burgdorf GPS: 45.27N, 115.91W ; Elevation 6115ft

*Getting Oriented*
- Take Forest Rd 246 off Warren Wagon Rd

*Activities*
- Burgdorf Hot Springs, 404 French Creek, 208-636-3036, www.burgdorfhotsprings.com, 10-8pm, $7pp

  Large pool at 100 degrees and smaller, hotter pools

*Lodging*
- Burgdorf Hot Springs, 404 French Creek, 208-636-3036, www.burgdorfhotsprings.com, 15 cabins no electricity or water, $35, some meals

  Cabins are rustic with wood stoves. Guests need to bring bedding, towels and anything else they need.

## Lucile GPS:45.32N, 116.18W ; Elevation: 1650ft

*Lodging*
- Steelhead Inn, 12212 Hwy. 95 S, 208-628-4279, steelheadinn.com, 9 rooms, some with kitchen, wifi, laundry, air con, continental breakfast

  Inn has a community kitchen for guest use, BBQ grills, a Gazebo and water front views. Motel rooms are simply decorated.

## Riggins GPS: 45.25N, 116.18W ; Elevation: 1821 ft

*Getting Oriented*
- Hwy. 95 along the Salmon River

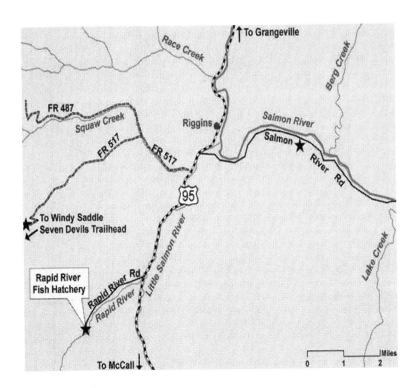

## Map of Riggins
(courtesy of fishandgame.idaho.gov)

*Practicalities*

- Library

  Salmon River Public Library, 126 N. Main St, 208-628-3394, 10-5pm, wifi

- Grocery

  Cloningers Family Foods, 104 N Main St, 208-628-3281

- Visitor Information

  rigginsidaho.com

  rigginsidaho.org

*Events*

- Hot Summer Nights, July

*Activities*

- Cleo Patterson Memorial City Park, Hwy. 95

- Exodus Wilderness Adventures,800-992-3484, www.exoduswildernessadventures.com, rafting, jet boat tours, fishing, kayaking, fishing, 1/2 day rafting $68, 1/2 day jet boat $90

- Heaven's Gate Lookout, 1/2m S of Riggins on hwy. 95 to Squaw Creek Rd and turn W 19 miles, wonderful Snake River overlook

- Heaven's Gate Outfitters, 1 Race Creek Rd, 208-628-2783, hgoadventures.com, hiking, rafting, horseback riding, fishing, hunting

- Lucile Recreation Site, 10m N of Riggins, drinking water, vault toilets, boat ramp

- Mountain River Outfitters, 411 N Main, 888-547-4837, idahoriver.com, rafting, full day rafting trip with lunch $95; 1/2 day $59

Trips are customized to the travelers

- River Adventures, 1310 S Main St, 800-524-9710, www.idahofishingus.us, fishing, jet boat tours,

- Rapid River Salmon Hatchery, 543 Rapid River Rd, 7m SW of Riggins, 208-628-3277, 8am-4pm

- Salmon River Challenge, 116 Time Zone Rd, 208-628-3264, www.salmonriverchallenge.com, rafting and fishing, half day $65, full day with lunch $95

- Salmon River Heritage Walking Tour, monument plaques posted around town explain the history of the town.

- Seven Devils Trail System, FR 517

- Shorts bar, 2m E of Riggins, picnic, no drinking water, vault toilets

- Wapiti River Guides, 128 N Main, 800-488-9872, www.doryfun.com, 1/2 day unique rafting or dory trips

## Dining

- Kate's Cattlemen's Restaurant, 601 South Main St, 208-628-3195

- Mountain River Outdoor Center Espresso, 411 N. Main, 208-628-3733

- River Rock Cafe, 1149 S Main St, 208, 6am-11pm, riverrockcafeandcatering.com, under $20

Hand formed burgers, biscuits and gravy, pizza and Italian Entrees, Burgers and salads.

- Seven Devils Steakhouse, 312 S Main St, 208-628-3558, facebook updated regularly, indoor and outdoor dining , 5-10pm

  Burgers, Fries

- Shellys Back Eddy Grill, 533 N Main, 208-628-9233, website doesn't work

- Summerville's Cafe, 106 S Main St, 208-628-3341, diner and steakhouse

- Two Rivers Coffee, 616 S Main St, 208-628-9222, tworiverscoffee.wordpress.com, facebook page updated regularly, 7am-4pm, wifi, indoor and outdoor seating

  Small wrought iron chairs and tables in the comfortable cafe.

## Camping
- Island Bar Recreation Site, 4m E of Riggins, boat launch, beach, portable toilet

- Pinehurst Resort Cabins & RV, 5604 Hwy. 95, 208-628-3323, www.pinehurstresort.us, cabins, full hookups, wifi,

  Cabins are heated and air conditioned and fully furnished

- River Village RV Park, 1434 N Hwy. 95, 208-628-3443, rivervillagervpark.com, showers, restrooms, pull thru, full hook, wifi, laundry

- Sites are located right along the river with attractive landscaping.

- Riverside RV Park, 1218 S Main, 208-628-3698, www.riversidervidaho.com, hook ups, wifi, pull thru, no showers

  Shady spacious park

- Shorts Bar Recreation Site, 2m E of Riggins, picnic tables, firepans, drinking water, vault toilets, boat ramp

## Lodging
- Big Iron Motel, 515 North Main ,208-628-3005, www.bigironmotel.com, hot tub, pets welcome, air con, wifi, rooms and suites

  Mostly remodeled rooms with simple decor

- Bunkhouse in Riggins, 208-628-3441, grouprate pricing $149 nightly for up to 8 people, wifi

Bunkhouse includes 3 bedrooms, 2 baths, kitchen and living room

- Serenity Lodge Bed & Breakfast, 402 Rapid River Rd, 6m from town, 208-628-4095, serenitylodgebandb.weebly.com, 2 rooms, indoor lap pool, sauna

Rooms are theme decorated each with private bath

- Mackay Bar ranch, 208-965-8355, www.mackaybarranch.com, reservations are required, $170pp for room, dinner and breakfast; $350pp for dinner, breakfast, lodging, horseback riding and all activities

Accommodations are in cabins or wall tents

- Mountain View Elk Ranch, trail rides, rafting, jet boat, hiking, campfire, wifi, $150pp for one night with breakfast and dinner, $675 two days, three nights

- Pinehurst Resort, 5604 Hwy. 95, MP 182, 208-628-3323, pinehurstresort.us, cabins with air con, RV, wifi, hookups, fishing, $65-105

Cabins have an eclectic decor with a mix of Oriental Carpets, velvet chairs and pitch forks or a red microwave.

- Riggins Motel, 615 S Main St, 800-669-6739, www.rigginsmotel.net, 2 and 4 people rooms, picnic area, bbq, wifi, hot tub, laundry

Furnishings are rustic lodge decor

- Riverview Motel, 708 N Hwy. 95, 888-256-2322, www.riverviewmotel.com , single and double rooms, wifi

Simple motel rooms, a private patio overlooking the river, picnic area and fire pit

- Salmon Rapids Lodge, 1010 S Main St, 208-628-2743, www.salmonrapids.com, indoor pool, hot tub, fireplace, full breakfast included, wifi, air con, rooms and suites, laundry

- Salmon River Motel, 1203 S Main St, 888-628-3025, www.salmonrivermotel.com , wifi, 1-3 room units, $39-100, laundry

- Shepp Ranch, French Creek, 208-382-4336, sheppranch.com, hot tub, sauna, river swimming, archery, horseback riding, fishing, jetboat tours, target shooting, $325pp per day,

Fresh baked, prepared meals, a friendly, comfortable lodge area, board games and books make for a comfy setting. Rustic cabins face the river and are carpeted with wood paneling and have private baths.

## Pollock GPS: 45.18N, 116.21W ; Elevation: 2333 ft

*Getting Oriented*

- Just off Hwy. 95 on Little Salmon River

*Activities*

- Northwest Voyageurs, 121 Old Pollock Rd, 800-727-9977, www.voyageurs.com, fishing, rafting, mountain biking, hiking

*Camping*

- Canyon Pines RV Resort, 159 Barn Rd, 866-744-4006, www.canyonpinesrv.com, 54 sites, wifi, restrooms, showers, laundry, rec room with microwave, piano, dump stations, country store

  Located along the Little Salmon River, very little shade.

*Lodging*

- Little Salmon Lodge, 121 Old Pollock Rd, 800-727-9977, www.littlesalmonlodge.com, 12 rooms with full breakfast included, wifi, hot tub, beer and wine bar, $109-149

## Adams County

## New Meadows GPS: 44.58N, 116.17 W ; Elevation: 3868 feet

*Getting Oriented*

- At the intersection of Hwy. 55 and Hwy. 95

*Practicalities*

- Visitor Center

  New Meadows Ranger District, 3674 Hwy. 95, 208-347-0300

- Library

  Meadows Valley Public Library, 400 Virginia, 208-347-3147

- Grocery

  Brown's Mountain Market, 302 Virginia St, 208-347-2306

Meadows Valley Market, 220 Virginia St, 208-347-2421

Pinehurst Trading Post Grocery, 5600 Hwy. 95, 208-628-3989

## Activities

- Dorsey War Memorial Park, Hwy. 95, playground, restrooms

- Historic Railroad Depot, 101 Commercial Ave, 208-347-2932, historicpindepot.com,

  Changing exhibits on local history

  *media connection: Video about the historic depot, http://idahoheritage.org/blog/2014/01/27/pin-railroad-depot-new-meadows/*

- The Last Resort, 5538 Hwy. 95, 208-628-3029, www.thelastresortoutfitter.com, fishing, rafting

- Lost Valley Reservoir, SW of New Meadows on Hwy. 95 and E on FR 89, dirt road, vault toilets, fishing, boating, interpretive trail

- Payette River Scenic Byway, Hwy 55/307 going West to Eagle Idaho, 112 miles

  The road follows the Payette River, passing Ponderosa State Park at McCall then past Lake Cascade, the Hembrey Creek Wetlands and over the Rainbow Bridge and Smith's Ferry ending in Eagle.

  *Media Connection: A brochure defining the Byway also provides a nice history of the route, file:///C:/Users/mvasudeva/Downloads/Payette_River_Scenic_Byway_CMP.pdf*

- Warren Brown Youth Park, North Commercial Ave, skate park

- Weiser River Trail, at E Main St and Cove Rd for parking, then follow E Main to the trail on Weiser River Rd, weiserrivertrail.webplus.net/index.html, 84m goes all the way to Weiser, restrooms along the way

  There are multiple parking options along Weiser River Rd

- Zims Hot Springs, 2995 Zims Rd, 208-347-2686, closed Monday, 103-106

  Developed pools, significant algae in the hot water pools

## Dining

- The Front Porch Cafe, 202 Norris Ave, 208-347-4343, seasonal, pit roasted bbq

- Granite Mountain Cafe, 213 Virginia St, 208-347-2513

- Roadhouse Java, 302 N Norris Ave, 208-347-2175, facebook page, 7am-7pm, coffee, hot chocolate, tea and light snacks

  Artistic coffee gallery

## Camping

- Cold Springs Campground, Hwy. 95S 8.6m to Lost Valley Reservoir Rd, 5000 ft elevation, 30 sites, dumping, fishing, boating, vault toilets, drinking water

  Campground is an open meadow lined with Ponderosa pines and about 3/4m from Lost reservoir. The Lost creek interpretive site is at the N end of the reservoir.

- Pinehurst Resort, 5604 Hwy. 95, MP 182, 208-628-3323, pinehurstresort.us, cabins, RV, wifi, hookups, fishing

## Lodging

- Hartland Inn, 211 N Norris Ave, 208-347-2104, thehartlandinn.com, motel and bed and breakfast

  3-Story brick mansion built in 1911 and with period decor and a carriage house. Motel rooms are typical low-end motel rooms.

- The Last Resort, 5538 Hwy. 95, 208-628-3029, www.thelastresortoutfitter.com, 3 rooms, fishing

- Meadows Valley Motel, 302 N Norris Ave, 208-347-2175, meadowsvalleymotel.com, 16 rooms, wifi,

## Tamarack GPS: 44.40N, 116.7 W ; Elevation: 4900 feet

Tamarack started in 2004 and has had an up and down history over the last 10 years with bankruptcy, arrest, auction, etc. Despite its struggles, the resort has managed to stay open except for one ski season and it has maintained a slow, steady development.

## Getting Oriented

- Tamarack is a small community on the west side of Lake Cascade off W. Mountain Rd.

## Activities

- Tamarack Canopy Zipline Tours, 311 Village Dr, 208-325-1006, www.tamarackzipline.com, $79-99

- Tamarack Resort, 311 Village Dr, 208-325-1000, tamarackidaho.com/, ski, snowboard, golf, zipline, bike, hike, raft, lessons and rentals

*Dining*

- Tamarack Resort, 311 Village Dr, 208-325-1000, tamarackidaho.com/, several restaurants but hours and dates change frequently. Check the website.

*Lodging*

- Tamarack Resort, 311 Village Dr, 208-325-1000, tamarackidaho.com/, ski, snowboard, golf, zipline, bike, hike, raft, wide array of lodging options from homes to lodge rooms to cottages, swimming pool, hot tub, lessons and rentals

   Easily the nicest place around but still in a state of incompleteness so services are limited. But the price of the resort is generally quite a deal for what you get, compared to other ski and golf resorts.

   Heads up: Tamarack has had lots of ups and downs. It's truly a beautiful place but do your due diligence.

## Council GPS: 44.43N, 116.26 W ; Elevation: 2927 feet

*Getting Oriented*

- Hwy. 95 runs through Council.

*Practicalities*

- Visitor Information

   Council Visitor Center, 108 Illinois Ave, Hwy. 95, 9am-5pm

   Council Ranger District Office, 2092 Hwy. 95, 208-253-0100

   www.councilidaho.org

- Grocery

   Council Valley Market, 202 Illinois Ave, 208-253-4421

   Ronnies Market, 102 Illinois, 208-253-4221

- Library

   Council Valley Free Library, 104 California Ave, 208-253-6004,

*Events*

- Council Mountain Music Festival, August, www.councilfestival.com

*Activities*

- Council Valley Museum, Hwy. 95, 208-253-4582, www.councilmuseum.com, 10-4pm, closed Mon, seasonal,

- Downtown Council City Park

- Weiser River Trail, trail access off N. Railroad and Hornet Creek Rd.

## Dining

- Branding Iron Steak House, 103 Illinois, 208-253-4499, under $20

- Steak, burgers, great broccoli cheddar soup, salads

- Council Mountain Cafe, 102 Moser, 208-253-4520

- One Eye Jack Pizza, 122 Illinois, 208-253-4951, 11-9pm

- Seven Devils Cafe , 116 Illinois Ave, 208-253-1177 (stiill here?)

- Shy Simon's Pizza, 406 Illinois Ave, 208-253-6233, 11-9pm

## Lodging

- Seven Devils Lodge Guest Ranch, Council Cuprum Rd, sevendevilslodge.com, 208-253-3014, 6 suites all with private bath, fishing, hiking, hunting, archery, $225pp per day all inclusive

- Elkhorn Bed and Breakfast, 1327 Hwy, 95, 208-741-2071, www.elkhornbnb.com, $85-130, wifi, pet friendly

  Rooms are a mix of Lodgepole pine and sleighbeds.

## Goodrich GPS: 44.39N, 116.33W; Elevation: 2772 ft

## Mesa GPS: 44.37N, 116.27W ; Elevation: 3251ft

### Getting Oriented

- Just to the West of Hwy. 95

## Indian Valley GPS: 44.33N, 116.26W ; Elevation: 3002ft

### Getting Oriented

- On Indian Valley Rd, to the East of Hwy. 95

### Dining

- Lakey Cafe, 1036 Hwy. 95, 208-256-4340

## Valley County

## McCall GPS: 44.54N, 116.6 W ; Elevation: 5013 feet

*Getting Oriented*
- On the S side of Payette Lake on Hwy. 55.

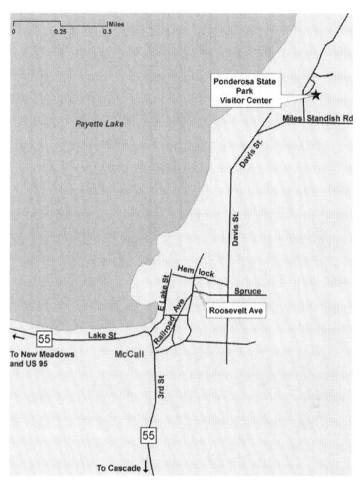

## Map of McCall

(courtesy of fishandgame.idaho.gov)

*Practicalities*
- Visitor Center

www.discovermccall.com

www.mccall.id.us

McCall Ranger District, 102 West Lake St, 208-534-0400

*Media Connection: stop in at the ranger station for an audio CD that takes visitors on a tour to Warren and its history*

- Grocery

  Aspen Market, 1609 Davis Ave, 208-634-7832

  City Market & Wine, 411 S 3rd St, 208-634-1919

  Paul's Market, 132 E Lake St, 208-634-8166, pauls.net, 6:30-11pm

  Ridley's Family Markets, 411 Deinhard Ln, 208-634-8719, shopridleys.com

- Library

  McCall Library, 218 E Park St, 208-634-5522

## Guides and Tours

- Backwoods Adventures, 411 Deinhard Ln, 208-469-9067, www.backwoodsadventuresmccall.com, canoe, kayak, Stand Up Paddle rentals

- Elk Springs Outfitters, 208-469-9999, www.mccalloutfitters.net, trail rides, fishing guides

- Payette Powder Guides, 208-634-6793, www.payettepowderguides.com, yurt rentals, guided ski tours, classes, Mt. Bike tours, rafting, vehicle shuttles

## Parks

- Art Robert's Park, 2nd St, municipal docks, picnic benches, swimming beach

- Brown Park, E Lake St & Hemlock St, shoreline path, benches, restrooms, picnic tables, playground

- Davis Beach, swimming area, restrooms, docks

- Disc Golf Course Nature Area, across from the High school

- Fish Pen Docks, at Brown Park

- Harshman Skateboard Park, 105-115 Idaho St, 208-634-3006

  Largest in Idaho

- Legacy Park, E Lake St, walking path, picnic tables, restrooms, swimming, boat ramp

- Rotary Park, E end of Lardo Bridge between Hwy. 55 & Payette Lake, beach, playground, restrooms, swimming, picnic tables

## *Fishing*

- Fly Fish McCall, 208-630-3863, flyfishmccall.com, guided trips and fishing classes

- McCall Fish Hatchery, 300 Mather Rd, 208-634-2690, 8am-4pm

## *Biking*

- bikemccall.com

- Rentals

  Gravity Sports, 503 Pine St, 208-634-8530, $15 half day, gravitysportsidaho.com, 9am-6pm

- Payette Powder Guides, www.payettepowderguides.com, Mt. Bike tours, half day $70, full day $85

  Mt bike half and full day tours with shuttle drop off and either a downhill ride or technical single track.

## *Hiking*

- Boulder Meadows Reservoir (Boulder Lake Trail #105), Hwy. 55S to Elo Rd, turn left then right on Farm to Market Rd, park your car below the reservoir and the trail goes along the North side, elevation 6269ft, 2m long trail with 700ft elevation gain, leads to other trails

- Box Lake Trail, Lick Creek Rd for 11m, 8m trail RT with 1900ft elevation change and lots of sun

- Dredge Pond/Ruby Meadows, 5m RT

- Goose Creek Falls (Powerline Trail), W on Hwy. 55 to Brundage Mountain turnoff for three miles, 2m RT with 680ft elevation change

  Trail winds down to the canyon to the Goose Creek Brdige to the junction with Goose Creek Trail #353

- East Fork Lake Fork Creek Trail, Lick Creek Rd past Little Payette Lake to Lake Fork Campground, trailhead is at the N side of the bridge, 2m with minimal elevation gain.

- Grass Mountain Lakes, take Brundage Rd N to Goose Lake Rd 7m past Goose Lake (20m from Hwy. 55), 7120ft elevation with 300 ft elevation gain, 2m hike to Grass Mountain lakes, fishing

  Trail goes through the Corral Fire of 1994

- McCall Pathway, this bike/hike path starts at Park St, just W of N. 3rd St and continues past the Highschool and the Cemetery and out past the airport and out of town to Donnelly (the pathway is not complete yet)

  *media connection: map of the McCall pathwayhttp://www.mccall.id.us/uploads/committees/pathways/documents/Valley_County_Pathways_Map.pdf*

- Payette Lakes Trail, Warren Wagon Rd, 3m route

- Secesh to Loon Lake, across the Rd from Ponderosa campground at the Secesh Bridge, trail goes 15m to Chinook Campground climbing 1500 feet

- Twin Lakes, Hwy. 55 W of town and turn on the Brundage Mountain Rd and take the Goose Lake/Hazard Lake turnoff past Goose Lake about 1 mile and take the road to the left for a short distance to a meadow, 6721ft elevation. Park

  Trail crosses a stream and climbs about 400ft.

## Culture and Arts

- Central Idaho Historical Museum, 1001 State St, 208-634-4497, www.centralidahohistoricalmuseum.com, 11-3 Wed-Thurs with house tour at 1:30, seasonal

  The museum is actually a collection of seven buildings built by the CCC in 1937. A variety of history exhibits are displayed.

## Scenic Byway

- French Creek Scenic Drive, Warren Wagon Rd (21) off Hwy. 55 27m past Lake Creek Bridge to gravel FR 246 left (sign to Riggins), 115m scenic loop

  This scenic route takes drivers past Payette Lake and North Beach State Park, Ponderosa State Park, North Beach State Park, fish spawning (seasonal), the Burgdorf Hot Springs, and climbs up through scenic views to Hwy. 95 at 71.5 miles turning left back to Hwy. 55.

## Boating and Rafting

- Rentals

Gravity Sports, 503 Pine St, 208-634-8530, $15 half day, gravitysportsidaho.com, 9am-6pm

- Hells Canyon Raft, 208-523-6502, www.hellscanyonraft.com, multi day trips

- McCall Lake Cruises, 203 E Lake St, 208-634-5253, mccalllakecruises.com

- Mile High Marina, 1300 E Lake St, 208-634-8605, milehighmarina.com, boat rentals, jet ski rentals, cafe

*Activities*

- Activity Barn Brundage Resort, 141 Moonridge Dr, 208-634-2222, tubing with a tow lift

- Bear Basin, 3m W on Hwy. 55, Nordic Trail system with 15 miles of groomed trails, lessons available, fee. Run by Payette Lakes Ski Club

- Brundage Mountain Resort, 3890 Gooselake Rd, 8m from McCall, 208-634-7669, www.brundage.com, 1800 vertical ft on 1500 acres with 320 base area inches annually, lessons and rentals, $58 daily lift ticket for adult

- Burgdorf Hot Springs, Warren Wagon Rd to Burgdorf Rd, 208-636-3036, www.burgdorfhotsprings.com, open 365 days a year, see separate listing for Burgdorf

- Gold Fork Hot Springs, 1026 Gold Fork Rd, East Roseberry Rd turns into Gold Fork Rd, 208-345-2456, goldforkhotsprings.com, 5000ft elevation, 10-10, closed Tues, fee, no power, port a pottie toilets, 94-108 degrees in developed pools

  Pools are natural formed, chlorine free

- Jug Mountain Ranch, 13834 Farm to Market Rd, Hwy 55 at Lake Fork and go east 1.5m on Lake Fork Rd, 208-630-4270, jugmountainranch.com, cross country skiing, snowshoeing, mountain biking

  Jug Mountain is a private residential community which offers some public recreation including 20m of hiking and mountain bike trails and 16m groomed Nordic trails. For a copy of their mountain biking map with separate double and single track trails market, download http://jugmountainranch.com/PDF/Trail%20Map_Summer_2012.pdf

- Little Ski Hill Alpine & Bear Basin Nordic Skiing, N Club Hill Blvd off Hwy. 55, drive E 8.5m to the hill, littleskihill.org, closed Mon, $15 adult, lessons, restrooms, nordic ski center is open every day 7days a week

405 ft of terrain and 30km of groomed cross country ski trails

Media Connection: Map of trails, http://littleskihill.info/wp-content/uploads/2013/12/BBNA.TrailMap.2013-2014.pdf

- Manchester Ice and Event Centre, 200 E Lake St, 208-634-3570, www.manchestericecenter.com

- Ponderosa State Park, 1920 N Davis Ave, 208-634-2164, 13m of groomed ski trails, snowshoe trails, dog park, yurt, fee, trail across the road

1000 acre peninsula located on Payette Lake

*Media Connection: Map of Ponderosa Park and Payette Lake (not a very good map) http://www.mccall.id.us/uploads/committees/pathways/documents/Ponderosa_Park_Trails_Map.pdf*

- Snowdon Wildlife Sanctuary Education and Visitor Center, 1981 Lick Creek Rd, 208-634-8050, www.snowdonwildlife.org,

Care of injured and orphaned wildlife. Visitors cannot enter the sanctuary itself but there is an education and visitor center.

## Coffee

- Moxie Java, 312 E Lake St, 208-634-3607, moxiejava.com

- Mountain Java, 501 Pine St, 208-634-2027, 6:30-6pm, lake views

Family run local coffee shop

- Wild River Java, 201 N 3rd St, 208-634-5282, drive thru

## Bakery and Treats

- Ice Cream Alley, 310 E Lake St, 208-634-1136

- Stacey Cakes, 136 E Lake St, 208-634-2537

Coffee, pastries and, of course, cakes

- Evening Rise, 303 Sunset St, 208-634-5031,

Artisan bread bakers and deli

## Dining

- Bistro 45, 1101 N 3rd St, 208-634-4515, www.bistro45mccall.com, occasional live music, wine and beer, 8am

Casual cafe with attractive brick patio. Salads, soups, and grilled sandwiches. Nice place for a mid-afternoon glass of wine and cheese plate.

- Blue Moon Outfitters, 208-634-3111, www.bluemoonyurt.com, December-March, $95pp

  Unique culinary adventure served up in Ponderosa State Park in a Yurt after snowshoeing to the location.

- Blue Moose Pizza, 907 W Lake St, 208-634-8646, bluemoosepizza.net

  Burgers, pizza, sandwiches, salad and breakfast. Also serves espresso.

- The Clubhouse Jug Mountain Ranch, Hwy 55 at Lake Fork and go east 1.5m on Lake Fork Rd, 208-630-4270, jugmountainranch.com/restaurant.html, 11-8pm, closed Tues. , under $20

  Steak, Pork, Pasta with upscale accompaniments.

- Crusty's Pizza, 214 Lenora St, 208-634-5005, facebook page updated regularly, 12-10pm, live music

  Italian food, pizza and live music. Some really unusual pizzas like Elk and Jalapeno make this a unique option.

- FoggLifter Cafe, 1003 N 3rd, 208-634-5507, 6am-6pm, coffee, breakfast, lunch

  Eggs Benedict, huevos Rancheros and a large variety of coffee/espresso drinks, Danishes and bagels.

- Growler's Pizza, 501 N 3rd St, 208-634-7755, growlerspizza.com, 11-9pm, under $20, 11-9, under $20

  Casual eatery serving casual pizza, burgers, wings type food. There is also a salad bar and focaccia sandwiches for the lighter side.

- Hometown Pizza, 337 Deinhard Ln, 208-634-2596, hometownpizzamccall.com, wine and beer, indoor and outdoor dining

  Pizza, sandwiches, wings and salad. Crusts and pizza sauce are made on site daily. Made to order slices for lunch.

- Lardo's Grill and Saloon, 600 W Lake St, 208-634-8191, lardogrillandsaloon.com, 11:30am-12, under $20

  Rustic, Western style dining with burgers, steak, chicken and lots of fried stuff. Italian dinners are also served with garlic bread and salad.

- *Lake Grill at Shore Lodge, 501 West Lake St, 800-657-6464, shorelodge.com/dining/lake-grill/, breakfast and lunch, 9am-3pm, under $20

  Known for burgers and huckleberry pancakes but has an eclectic menu with lamg and lentil stew, northwest nachos or Asian tuna salad. Probably the nicest place for lunch in town. Breakfast is a mix of traditional (Eggs Benedict) and more unusual like Smoked Idaho Trout Hash.

- McCall Brewing Co, 807 N 3rd St, 208-634-3309, mccallbrew.com, 11-9pm, under $20

  Burgers, burritos and a variety of entrees like Blackened Chicken or Fettuccine Alfredo. You can also get lots of fried stuff like fried jalapenos

- My Father's Place, 901 N 3rd St, 208-634-4401, indoor and outdoor seating

  Burgers, fries and shakes

- Pueblo Lindo, 1007 W Lake St, 208-634-2270, 11-10pm, facebook page updated regularly, full bar, under $15

  Huge menu of traditional and regional Mexican items including Mole.

- Rupert's Restaurant, 1101 N 3rd St, 208-634-8108, rupertsathotelmccall.com, 5-8:30, closed Tues-Weds, under $20, full bar, under $30

  Lakeside dining with seasonal menu that features such items as Elk Carpaccio, Idaho Trout, risotto fritters.

- Salmon River Brewery, 411 Railroad Ave, 208-634-4SRB, salmonriverbrewery.com,

  Pub type food like hot dogs, fish and chips, baked pretzels and beer and cheese soup.

- Stax Sandwiches, 802 N 3rd, 208-634-8193, under $15

  Huge sandwiches with fresh bread in a casual atmosphere

- Steamer's Steak & Seafood, 308 E Lake St, 208-634-1411, steamersrestaurant.com, 5-9pm, under $30, wine and beer

  Fish and steak served with salad and potatoes.

- The Pancake House, 209 N 3rd St, 208-634-5849, mccallpancakehouse.com, 6am-9pm, under $15, wifi

Breakfast served all day. Huge plates of American comfort food like chicken and dumplings, deep fried chicken, burgers or nachos.

- Toll Station Pizza & Pasta, 409 Railroad Ave, 208-634-7818, tollstationpizza.com, 11-10pm, great outdoor deck, under $20, beer and wine

  Pizza and salad, burgers and pasta.

- The Narrows at Shore Lodge, 501 W Lake St, 208-634-2244, 5:30-10, under $40

  Frequently changing menu in a decidedly upscale restaurant probably the nicest in town. Pheasant, Porterhouse, Alaskan Halibut all served a la carte. Views from the restaurant look out over the lake so it's worth eating here in the daylight.

*Lodging*
- Chains include Best Western, Holiday Inn, Super 8

- Bear Creek Lodge, 3492 Hwy. 55, 208-634-3551, www.bearcreeklodgemccall.com, cabins, lodge rooms and house, campfire pit, breakfast included, hot tub

  Rooms are sparsely decorated with wood accents and simple comfortable furnishings. A great room and deck are available for guest use.

- Hotel McCall, 1101 N Third St, 866-800-1183, www.hotelmccall.com, 19 rooms and suites, continental breakfast, $200-350

- The Hub Mountain House, 1308 Roosevelt Ave, 208-315-2500, thehubmountainhouse.com, 2 suites, hot tub, wifi, breakfast included, $150

- Shore Lodge, 501 West Lake St, 800-shorelodge.com, rooms, cottages and suites, wifi, sandy beach, outdoor pool, tennis, fitness center, mountain bike rentals, $250

# Payette Lake GPS: 41.31N, 120.10 W ; Elevation: 5000 feet

*Getting Oriented*
- On the N edge of McCall, this 5330 acre glacial lake was carved over 10,000 years ago

*Practicalities*
- Visitor Center

  Ponderosa Park Visitor Center, 1920 N Davis Ave, 208-634-2164

- Restrooms

    Ponderosa Park, North Beach

*Activities*
- Listed in Order starting from Hwy. 55 at the S. end of the lake and following Lake St East

    Mile High Marina (see in McCall listing)

    Davis Beach

    Ponderosa State Park, see listing under McCall

    Pilgrim Cove

    North Beach, see under McCall

# Lake Fork GPS:44.49N, 116.05W ; Elevation 4974ft

*Getting Oriented*
- Hwy. 55, S of McCall.

*Practicalities*
- Grocery

    2 Sisters Country Store, 13844 Hwy. 55, 208-634-6375, 7am-7pm

*Camping*
- Lake Fork Campground, 9m E of McCall on Lick Creek Rd, vault toilet, potable water, picnic tables, fire pits, several trails are accessible here

# Donnelly GPS: 44.43N, 116.43 W ; Elevation: 4865 feet

*Getting Oriented*
- Hwy. 55.

*Practicalities*
- Shopping

    Roseberry General Store, 2511 Roseberry Rd, 208-325-5000, roseberrygeneralstore.com, May-Sept, Built in the early 1900's, the store is restored with all its old grandeur selling a combination of old fashioned and contemporary goods including toys and penny candy.

- Library

Donnelly Library, 150 East St, 208-325-8237.,

## Activities

- Roseberry General Store and Museum, 2511 Roseberry Rd, 208-325-5000, roseberrygeneralstore.com, May-Sept, Built in the early 1900's, the store is restored to its original grandeur.

- Roseberry Townsite, 1m E of Donnelly on East Roseberry, area is open to visitors 24/7 but buildings have various hours.

  Townsite includes many buildings built in the early 1900's under various levels of reconstruction. There is also a Finnish Homestead

- Valley County Museum, 13131 Farm to Market Rd (off Roseberry Rd), 208-325-8628

## Dining

- *Buffalo Gal, 319 N Main, 208-325-8258, buffalogalidaho.com, under $20, beer and wine

  Wide variety of options in this small town cafe. Ice cream is made in house. Menu is quite diverse with Argentinean Beef, BBQ buffalo, spaghetti and meatballs and Hungarian pork Chop

- Main Street Pizza, 127 N Main, 208-325-4040, 11-9pm

  Sandwiches, pizza and salad

- *Donnelly's Flight of Fancy, 282 N Main St, 208-325-4432, www.dessertjunkies.com, 7am-5pm, closed Sun, bakery, breakfast and lunch

  Homemade soup and sandwiches on in-house baked bread. Cookies, brownies, pies and cakes. Breakfast is quiche, oatmeal or a breakfast sandwich.

## Camping

- Chalet RV Park, 418 S Main St, 208-325-8223, www.g7rvresorts.com/idaho/chalet, 76 sites, showers, restrooms, laundry, wifi

- Donnelly Boat Dock and Campgrounds, bathroom, fire pits, picnic tables

- SISCRA's Willow Creek Campground, S of Donnelly, 208-325-8130, 198 sites, hook ups, dump station, restrooms with hot showers, limited wifi, seasonal, boat launch, fishing, picnic tables, pets are welcome

*Lodging*
- Boulder Creek Inn, 629 Hwy. 55, 208-325-8638, www.thebouldercreekinn.com, 43 rooms and suites, wifi, laundry

- Long Valley Motel, 161 S Main St, 208-325-8271, facebook page, $75-95, wifi

**Cascade** GPS: 44.30N, 116.2W ; Elevation: 4760ft

*Getting Oriented*
- On the SE side of Lake Cascade on Hwy. 55.

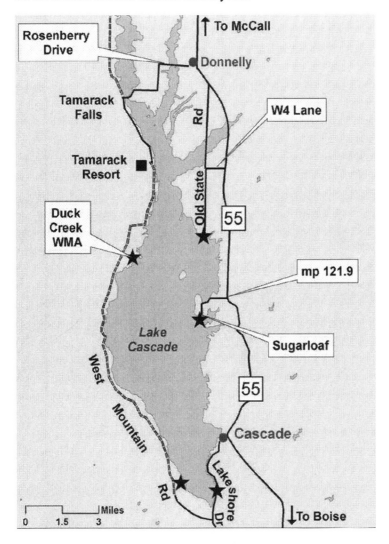

## Map of Cascade
(courtesy of fishandgame.idaho.gov)

*Practicalities*

- Visitor Information

  Info Depot, 750 S Main, 208-405-3000, www.kellyswhitewaterpark.com

  www.cascadechamber.com

- Grocery

  D-9Grocery, 102 S Main, 208-382-4215

- Library

  Cascade Public Library, 105 N Front St, 208-382-4757.,

*Events*

- Valley County Rodeo, August

*Activities*

- *Kelly's Whitewater park, 750 S Main, 208-405-3000, www.kellyswhitewaterpark.com, free, paddle boarding, river surfing, tubing, canoing, 2.5m river trail, fishing, museum

  This is a lovely place to stop for an introduction to Cascade. It's located right on the Payette River and a visitor center and museum offer exhibits on history.

- Cascade Raft, 208-793-2221, www.cascaderaft.com, rafting and floating half ($45) and full ($85) day.

- Cascade-Smith's Ferry Area Hiking Trails, 8m S of Cascade, go E on FR 409 about 3m to FR 417 3m to FR 417B 3m

- Gear and Grind, 762 South Main St, 208-382-6580, www.gearandgrind.com, kayak, paddleboard, tube and raft rentals

- Lake Cascade State Park, 970 Dam Rd, 208-382-6544, camping available, boating, fishing, biking, swimming

  *Media Connection: Information, including maps, available, http://parksandrecreation.idaho.gov/parks/lake-cascade*

- *Snowbank Mountain, S on Hwy. 55 take Cabarton Rd 6m to Snowbank Rd (446) to the right for 11m (plan at least 2 hours for the RT drive), open June 1-Oct 31, 8322ft elevation, restrooms on the route, trails, vault toilets on the drive

  Great views on the unpaved but well maintained drive to the twin-summited mountain at 8300ft.

Blue Lake Trail (#119), 1m easy trail through a meadow

Tripod Trail, 3m walk to top along the ridge

- *The Strand, starting at Water's Edge RV Park at the N end of town ending at Fischer Pond Park, 2.5m trail

  The path winds along the North Fork of the Payette River and can be accessed off Sawyer St at many points.

  *Media Connection: Nice brochure done by a local organization about this pathway, http://dw381979td36g.cloudfront.net/upload/6122/vc-pathways-spring-2011-newsletter-final-online.pdf*

- Whitewater Expeditions, Five Mile Bar, 208-382-4336, www.whitewaterexpeditions.com, fishing, tours of the Salmon River, shuttles

## Dining

- Cascade Store Ice Cream & Candy, 101 N Main, 208-382-3101, www.thecascadestore.com, 10-5:30pm

- Gramma's Restaurant, 224 N Main St, 208-382-4602

  American home-style food and salad bar

- Lakefront Steak House, 117 Lake Shore Dr, 208-382-4990

- Reo's Pizza, 402 S Main, 208-382-5100, delivery

  Family pizza place with arcade, salad bar and taco bar

- Route 55 Cafe and Drive In, 806 S Main, 208-382-4496

- Wheeler's Pharmacy-Coffee Counter, 104 N Main St, 208-382-4700

- Whistle Stop Cafe, 109 N Main, 208-382-4700, beer and wine

  Pizza, burgers and homemade bread

## Camping

- Arrowhead RV Park, 955 S Hwy. 55, 208-382-4534, www.arrowheadpark.com, wifi, walking trails, dumping, showers, rustic camping cabins and yurts

- Water's Edge RV Park, 800-574-2038, watersedgervpark.com, pull thru, hook ups

  On the Payette River

*Lodging*

- Alpine Cottage Motel, 519 N Main St, 208-382-4800, cascadevacation.com, 4 units

- The Ashley Inn, 500 N Main, 208-382-5621, theashleyinn.com, 67 rooms and suites, pool, full breakfasts, $150-300

  Decor is floral and pastel in a big way, fireplaces in all rooms, some with four poster beds and all individually decorated.

- Bears Knight Inn, 208-382-4370, www.bearsknightinn.com, $55-65, wifi

  Country decor

- Birch Glen Lodge, 726 Hwy. 55, 208-382-4238, birchglenlodge.com, 27 units, wifi

  Common area in the lodge for all visitors to use.

- Pinewood Lodge, 900 S Hwy. 55, 208-382-4800, thepinewoodlodge.com, 10 units, small pets welcome, $55 and up

  Basic motel rooms

- Wapiti Meadow Ranch, 1667 Johnson Creek Rd, 1 1/2hr from Cascade, 208-633-3217, wapitimeadowranch.com, cabins with full kitchens, fishing, $100

- Warm Lake Lodge, 175 N Shoreline Dr, 26m E of Cascade, 208-632-2000, northshorelodgeidaho.com, cabins with kitchen, laundry, boat rentals, restaurant on site, $86-120

  Cabins are simple and rustic

## Yellow Pine GPS: 44.57N, 115.29W ; Elevation: 4802ft

*Getting Oriented*

- Like Creek Rd to E Fork Rd from Hwy. 55

*Practicalities*

- Yellow Pine General Store, 315 Yellow Pine Ave, 208-633-3300,

*Events*

- Yellow Pine Music and Harmonica Festival, yellowpinemusicandharmonicafestival.org, August

*Activities*
- Yellow Pine Backcountry Historical Museum, yellowpinemuseum.org, open with advance notice

  Volunteer run, this small museum in a school house has history exhibits

*Dining*
- Silver Dollar Grill, 345 Yellow Pine Ave, 208-633-6207, 6am-10pm

*Camping*
- Yellow Pine Campground, FR 413A, 14 sites, drinking water, vault toilets

*Lodging*
- Alpine Village Lodge, 208-385-0271, kitchens, laundry, RV hookups, $35-75

- Yellow Pine General Store, 315 Yellow Pine Ave, 208-633-3300, 2 cabins for rent

**Smiths Ferry** GPS: 44.18N, 116.05W ; Elevation: 4554ft, nothing here

**Genesee** GPS: 46.33N, 116.55W ; Elevation: 2680ft

*Getting Oriented*
- Off Hwy. 95

*Practicalities*
- Library

  Genesee Community Library, 140 East Walnut St, 208-285-1398

- Grocery

  Food Center, 216 W Chestnut, 208-285-1323

*Activities*
- White Spring Ranch, 1004 Lorang Rd, 208-416-1006, whitespringranch.org, facebook page updated regularly, Sun and Tues 1-5pm and by appointment

  National Historic Site being restored to its 1885 origins.

*Dining*
- Brass Lantern Restaurant and Corner Bar, 153 W Walnut, 208-285-1512

## Media Guide to the Region

- Maps

  An Atlas of Idaho is an excellent aid for traveling anywhere off the beaten path in Idaho (which is most of the state). There are two main options: The Delorme Atlas and the Benchmark Maps Idaho Road and Recreation Atlas. They are both fairly comprehensive but the Benchmark is more detailed.

- General Information

  Outdoor Idaho, a series of videos on outside adventures in Idaho covering everything from beautiful scenery to encounters with animals, video.idahoptv.org/program/outdoor-idaho/

  Idaho fish and game department also does videos of wildlife and regional areas, fishandgame.idaho.gov/is/media/video

  imnh.isu.edu/digitalatlas/aboutus/about.htm

  > Excellent Website on Idaho history, geology and geography as well as flora and fauna. Very complete.

Flora Fauna

  Idaho: Wildlife Viewing Guide, Aimee L Pope, 2003

  Birds of Idaho Field Guide, Stan Tekiela, 2003

  Idaho Trees & Wildflowers: A Folding Pocket Guide, James Kavanagh, 2010

  Idaho Birds: A Folding Pocket Guide, James Kavanagh, 2002

  Idaho Mountain Wildflowers: A Photographic Compendium, Scott Earle, 2001

  Idaho Wildlife: A Folding Pocket Guide, James Kavanagh, 2011

Guidebooks

  Backcountry Roads-Idaho, Lynna Howard, 2008. This is a beautiful book with limited travel information.

  Flyfisher's Guide to Idaho, Ken Retallic, 2013

  Mountain Biking in McCall, Steve Stuebner, 2010

  Trails of the Sawtooth and White Cloud Mountains, Margaret Fuller, 2011

Trails of the Frank Church: River of No Return Wilderness, Margaret Fuller, 2002

Scenic Driving Idaho, Bob Clark, 1998

The Hiker's Guide to McCall & Cascade, Scott Marchant, 2011

The Day Hiker's Guide to Stanley Idaho, Scott Marchant, 2009

Hiking Idaho, 2nd Ed, Jackie Maughan, 2001

Roadside Geology of Idaho, David D Alt, 1989

Kids

My First Book About Idaho, Carole Marsh, 2000

P is for Potato: An Idaho Alphabet Book, Stan Steiner, 2005

The Incredible Idaho Coloring Book, Carole Marsh, 2001

Mountain Men of Idaho, Darcy Williamson, 2011

Idaho: The Gem State, Marcia Amidon Lusted, 2010

History

www.nezperce.com, information and education

Roadside History of Idaho, Betty B Derig, 1996

It Happened in Idaho, Randy Stapilus, 2002

Idaho Echoes in Time: Traveling Idaho's History and Geology, R. G. Robertson

Made in the USA
San Bernardino, CA
16 June 2018